Fragments of My Life

Also by Carol J. Griffin

Straight From the Heart—Poetry
Rituals—Ways to Heal the Spirit
Since I Met You—Poetry

Fragments of My Life

✦

A Journal About Manic Depression And Its Companion Illnesses

Carol J. Griffin

iUniverse, Inc.
New York Lincoln Shanghai

Fragments of My Life
A Journal About Manic Depression And Its Companion Illnesses

iUniverse, Inc.

For information address:
iUniverse, Inc.
2021 Pine Lake Road, Suite 100
Lincoln, NE 68512
www.iuniverse.com

ISBN: 0-595-28905-3

Printed in the United States of America

For my son,

Thomas M. Richert

who sometimes has to parent me

Contents

INTRODUCTION 1

POEM: FRAGMENTS OF MY LIFE 3

MANIA 4

DEPRESSION 7

MEETING MYSELF 10

ATTORNEY KAYE 11

LIFE WITH UNDIAGNOSED MANIC DEPRESSION AND
    ATTENTION DEFICIT DISORDER 13

BILLY GRAHAM. 15

TOM 17

THE BETRAYAL. 19

FRAGMENTS 1957–1974

COLLEGE 25

NANCY 26

SUICIDE 28

CHRISTMAS. 30

NEW ORLEANS 32

BROWN COUNTY, INDIANA 33

AVON 35

HIGH MOODS 36

DICK 38

FRAGMENTS 1974–1985

FLORENCE LITTLE 43

GLENDA COX 45

I JOINED THE RESERVES (ALMOST) 47

DESPAIR AND THE CHURCH 48

COURT CLERK 49

TACO BELL KITCHEN 51

HYSTERECTOMY 52

DR. WILLIS 54

DR. WILLIS AND THE DIAGNOSIS 56

FRAGMENTS 1985–Present

HONG KONG 61

SUSAN SMITH 64

CHARLES 66

DR. KATZ 69

DAVE 73

ATTENTION DEFICIT DISORDER 76

JIM 78

ATTORNEY KAYE 81

ATTORNEY KAYE—THE HEARING 82

DECISION—THEN APPEAL 84

EDUARDO 88

FINAL APPEAL 90

EDUARDO AND A TRIP TO NEW YORK CITY 92

STREET PEOPLE 94

HELPFUL SUGGESTIONS 96

CONCLUSION 99

INTRODUCTION

I have written this book to help people living with bipolar mood disorder, caused by a lack of enough serotonin to the brain, and people who experience Attention Deficit Disorder as a companion illness and their families. It is my intention to write about my life, six decades of this illness, to inform others this is not a character disorder, but a very real illness stemming from a malfunctioning brain.

I will describe episodes from my life, which I call fragments, to help clarify the illness. I would like the reader to understand the word depression when it describes a medical condition, Manic Depression (lack of serotinum to the brain) as opposed to depression brought on by circumstance.

On my sixtieth birthday last month, I walked along a Florida beach enjoying the beauty of the Gulf watching the birds wading in and out of the green water. This was a place I felt comfortable and so I sat down on the sand and thought about those six decades. I thought about my children, my marriages, and this illness and how it has taken so much of my joy and dignity. I was glad I made the decision to live in Florida after growing up in New York City, and then living in Illinois where I felt like an unwelcome guest. I have traveled to Europe and Asia, seen most of the California Coast and most of the Northeast. I love to travel.

I was successful in keeping my children with me instead of giving custody to their father, a minister and convicted criminal, but I paid a price. I worked for 24 years with an illness that sometimes led to my dismissal. I never thought of leaving the children even during times when they took advantage of me because of my illness.

I've studied Christianity at the college level. I moved on in my quest to find favor with God and be relieved of this illness. I have written about my beliefs perhaps, in an unorthodox manner, and they are contained in this book.

Everything written here is filtered through my reality. I am not a health care professional. However, I am a survivor of an illness so devastating that it invites criticism and contempt and places blame on the victim.

I have two children. Tom is 40 and married to Dina. He attended Harvard Graduate School. Kathleen is 36 and married to Arturo. They are both college graduates, have two children, Sammy and Soleil.

I love my family very much, and I know they have been observers of my illness more than have been supporters. However, my son's help in recent years has been so necessary at times and I appreciate all he has done for me. I think most people do not understand and so for them and all the other family members and friends I have written this book.

FRAGMENTS OF MY LIFE

In the fragments of my life I seek to integrate my needs
Tucked in the narrow spaces between thoughts and deeds

To gain approval I try to cast this beautiful illusion
As I succeed it serves to trap me in endless confusion

Lured and encouraged by the praises of my potential
I push on, set goals, make plans, missing what is essential

Promising performances I will never be able to achieve
I'm lost, a disappointment, I am my own bereaved

All of life is an illusion, I strive to cast my own Camelot
When the truth is revealed, who I am is who I'm not

                                        Carol J. Griffin

MANIA

I often wonder how many of the people who try to climb Mt. Everest or bungee jump are not suffering from a prolonged case of mania. I describe this as a belief in their infallibility and their need for a chronic high. We read a lot about shopping and over shopping and compulsive shopping and while this is characteristic of mania it is also characteristic of a large percentage of people in this country who do not suffer from Manic Depression. However, the credit card is especially dangerous to manic-depressive Illness. While this can be attributed to mania in some cases the need to take a chances is prevalent in other areas of life which can lead one into dangerous situations. The desire to speed, use equipment with no knowledge of how is works or perhaps the most dangerous, a poor choice of friends.

In manic depression the belief system is constantly having to readjust and somehow find peace in reality, but more than likely the cycle will begin again. It picks and chooses its own time and it will stay for a day or for years.

Most people have a pattern. I rapid cycle which enabled me to remain in the work force for 24 years. By the time someone would suspect there was a problem I could be back to normal. On days when I was depressed to the point of being unable to function I would call in sick and lie in bed crying.

I too have my manic times. I rearrange furniture with a super strength born of mania. I have moved a large cherry hutch as I turned my living room into a decorator's dream. I would paint whole rooms at 2:00 a.m., and go grocery shopping in the middle of the night. I had endless energy.

My form of mania has also manifested itself in relationships, destructive ones. The answer for me is to avoid relationships. In my case most of the men who I told about my illness went right to denial. "There is nothing wrong with you," they say. They have no interest in emotionally supporting me.

I've dated two retired police officers. They both were alcoholics. One put a gun to my head when I told him I didn't want to see him any more. The other man I met in a mental hospital. How I rationalized this is beyond me. He became possessive. He had just bought a new car. He came over to show me the car and said he would take me to work. On the way to work we were in a four-car pile up. He was arrested for driving while intoxicated.

I broke up with him and he demanded every gift be returned. At first I declined as a matter of principle, but when he broke down my door I decided to give him everything. He sent me a note threatening my life every day for a year. The police told me there was nothing they could do unless he killed me. He eventually moved away from the area and I haven't heard from him again.

One has to live with the consequences of mania once reality sets in. This mood is the greatest deceiver and while elation seems wonderful at the time it can cause as much damage as depression.

WINNING THE LOTTERY   MANIC

DEPRESSION

When one is chemically depressed life loses all rhythm and the desire to flourish is replaced with lethargy. Life is confusing and your thoughts have no meaning. You want to hide in bed, but can't always accommodate this need. As an example recently I found myself in the first real depressive episode I had experience in a few months. I had to go to the grocery store but I felt unable to do so. Every thing about it frightened me. When should I go, now or later? Will I remember my list? Will I see someone I know? What shall I wear?

I misplaced the list three times. I thought of waiting until the next day, but, the next day would be the same and in the meantime I would continue to agonize over it, so I left to accomplish mission impossible.

The supermarket felt like an obstacle course as I darted up one isle and then down the other. I had lost my list and for a moment thought I could not go on without it. I was breaking into a sweat and my heart was beating rapidly. I decided it was time to check out.

When I returned from the store, I didn't feel safe until the door was locked from the inside. I put the perishables away, grabbed an afghan and buried myself on the sofa. I slept for three hours and when I awoke it was dark outside. I felt as if all my energy has been drained from me. Confusion comes and goes. Panic is no stranger here.

In the evening I looked in the closet where I always hang my purse. It was not there. I looked around the condominium and when I did not see it I went down to my car. It was not in the car. I ran for the elevator as I remember I had been in a bookstore the day before and had the purse on the back of my chair. I tried to call the bookstore, but I kept dialing and getting a wrong number. I got the operator to dial the call and I got music. I decided to hold and a woman answered eventually. I told her about my purse. She checked with lost and found, but no purse had been turned in. I hung up the phone and cried. I was shaking. All the credit cards, my license, my checkbook and Christmas cash were gone. What I did not remember was I had the purse at the grocery store that day.

I could not think of anyone to call. I went into the bedroom, which was a total disaster. I was looking for a tissue when I saw two white pillow shams on the floor with what looked like something red between them. It was my purse. This episode in my life was brought to you courtesy of Manic Depression and Attention Deficit Disorder (ADD). I call them the dynamic duo. I got depressed and didn't stay within my routine. I am usually very neat but this day I was depressed I did not have the ability to complete my routine.

Depression takes my life force away from me. Nothing is real. My mind can't organize the smallest tasks. There is a sinking feeling in my stomach, as if something awful is going to happen to lock me in this mood forever. I feel nothing will ever be the same for depression traps me in the past and the present has no meaning and I feel I have no future except to repeat this experience again and again. The days go by slowly. My bed becomes my only refuge. Some times I sleep and this is my escape and when I can't sleep I think about death as my escape. Gradually I'll pull out of it. The truth is my life takes places not in my moods but in the spaces between my moods.

MEETING MYSELF

In some ways I feel as if I've lived three lives, manic, depressed, and the real me sandwiched in between, only to be over shadowed by a person I am not. Once in a while I get the privilege of meeting my real self, not the high over-spender who gives a way friendship to everyone she speaks to, who comes up with great ideas that can't be accomplished, and who over commits and then lets people down. Nor is my real self the person who can't cope if there is a change in plans, who gets anxiety attacks, and at sixty years of age still has abandonment issues and takes to her bed when depressed. The real me is generous in spirit and with her resources, loves her family, and willingly do things for others.

ATTORNEY KAYE

Seated in Mr. Kaye's law office I waited with apprehension to meet the man who to a large extent would be responsible for the outcome of my Disability Hearing. I wondered if I was doing the right thing by filing for disability and admitting defeat after 24 years of working. I knew manic depression would keep me from working for periods of days and in recent times for a week or more.

This was further complicated by the advent of computers and my Attention Deficit Disorder, which made it difficult for me to navigate in the computer and resulted in a loss of productivity. I would forget which screen I was using. I would check my notes, but was often unable to understand them. Sometimes I would get help from co-workers, but in time they would walk away in disgust.

I did not have to wonder how this happened to me. This is a genetic brain disease found on my father's side of the family. I thought I could beat it and spent a great deal of time and money looking for a medicine that would make me like other people. I started to think about my father. In later years he was awarded disability. He was often depressed or agitated. I tried to stay out of his way and so did my brother. During World War II we were forced to live on the Lower East Side of Manhattan with my grandmother. My father, a German immigrant and a citizen of the United States, was let go when the company he worked for started engaging in defense work.

After the war my father was able to return to his trade. My parents began to talk about buying a house, but I did not think it would happen. My mother found something wrong with every house we looked at. We went to Maine the summer I turned nine. I felt very sad watching my mother scribble out a note to my father telling him we would be back at the end of the summer. My mother was punishing my father for his illness. By leaving she caused him to feel separation anxiety. When we did return to New York City my father met the train. He was smiling, which was very rare. My father had put a down payment on a beautiful white house on Long Island. My mother made his life hell, but he prevailed. This was the only time I saw my father happy and this was the only time he acted on his own. It has taken me many years to appreciate the sacrifices my father made for us. He endured three different modes of transportation, a twelve-hour day, and the constant mood swings so we could live in a beautiful place. He used to have an easy thirty-minute commute to work and now he had a long commute.

After getting over the excitement of the new house things returned to normal. My mother was still the sloppy housekeeper she always had been. My father, who was obsessed with neatness, and her battled over this issue every night until my father left the table and sat in his chair. As I look back I wonder why he stayed. He could have rented a furnished room and taken a part time job, but he stayed for all of us so we might have a chance to live in a nice house in a good neighborhood and have a decent life. Even though he was often unhappy or withdrawn I feel he demonstrated the real meaning of love by stretching his ability. I don't believe he ever kissed me. He would shake hands with my brother and me on Christmas Day and that was our physical contact for the year.

Mr. Kaye opened the door to his office and motioned for me to come in. I had been reflecting on the past and now I made an emotional shift into the present. Mr. Kaye sat behind his desk. He was average height and weight. His features were sharp, he wore glasses, appeared to be about fifty. He looked at me for about thirty seconds. "I'm supposed to prove you are disabled?" he said. I was wearing a dress I wore to work. *This seemed to me* the proper way to go to a law office. I would soon find out, the hard way, disability was one big costume party. In my family the mentally ill do crazy neatly.

Mr. Kaye went over my history, medical and work. He asked no questions. He noted I had twenty-two jobs in the last year. I had to sign releases and fifteen minutes later I was dismissed. I had no money or savings and I had no job. The thought of going on welfare made me feel ill. I felt alone.

LIFE WITH UNDIAGNOSED MANIC DEPRESSION AND ATTENTION DEFICIT DISORDER

I began to realize I was not like other people when I was about 16 years old. It was a vague feeling, nothing I could describe. It never occurred to me I could be suffering from the same genetic illness my father had. He never missed a day of work, leaving the house at 6:00 a.m. and arriving home at 7:00 p.m.

He was a depressed man and this could sometimes take the form of agitated depression. He would find fault with almost everything and my mother compounded the problem by turning each remark into a new game I called "Up-Roar." Most of the time my father did not speak even when spoken to unless it was vital.

We had a car for a few years. When the four of us and the dog were ready to go my father would get out of the car, go back in the house and check to see that nothing was plugged in, and that the faucets were all off. He went from the attic to the basement. He would repeat this three times. We would wait impatiently in the car. The dog would cry softly then bark when he saw my father return to the car. Once this ritual was completed we could leave.

My father did not like to talk to people or engage in any conversation, so it came as a surprise when his short comment may have contributed to my cousin's broken engagement. He did not like to visit people. He would find a corner and drink a glass of beer. He would try not to interact with people. My aunt brought out a lovely tablecloth made by my cousin, the future bride. The women were admiring it and one of my aunts said, "You will be good at darning socks." My cousin's future mother-in-law looked shocked. She said, "Bruce never wore a darned sock." Without missing a beat my father said, "He wore socks with holes in them?" My family burst into laughter. The next day the engagement was broken. There was a limit to my father's wit, making this a rare occasion.

13

As I became an adult I would find myself in the same situation as my father. I would fixate on some unimportant thing and vent my behavior through agitated depression. This is not to suggest my illness was caused by an unpleasant childhood. It was not. This is a genetic disorder many of the members of my father's family have inherited. I was born with this illness. This concept is very difficult for the public to accept. It is considered bad behavior when you are struggling with Manic Depression or any form of mental illness.

I often wonder why there is a need for people to attach the illness to events in life rather than place blame on the illness itself. This kind of depression is not to be associated with some negative event. In reality the person does not know why he is depressed. The culprit here is the brain and its lack of enough serotonin.

It is this imbalance in the brain that corresponds to the imbalance in the pancreas causing diabetes. However, the acceptance of these illnesses by the public is very different. You can tell people you have diabetes and they are sympathetic. You can tell people you are mentally ill and they will avoid you. Yet, celebrities raise money and actively admit they have diabetes.

Some brave women, such as Patty Duke, Kristy McNichols, Connie Francis, and Carrie Fisher have gone public, but there is still the need for commentators to attach the mental illness to events in their career. In my opinion the illness gave them the drive and ability to keep going and going and make them stars. I believe the vast majority of people in this country have an inaccurate concept of mental illness. First comes the illness, then comes the behavior.

BILLY GRAHAM

At the age of 16 I took the train from Queens to Manhattan to attend the Billy Graham Crusade. I walked towards Madison Square Garden on this warm summer evening with no way of knowing how this evening would impact my life for decades. Madison Square Garden was filled with people. I found a seat in the balcony and waited eagerly to see and hear Billy Graham. After the choir sang and we prayed Billy Graham was introduced. He was very well groomed, and had a magnetic personality. One could feel the energy of the crowd shift.

He began to speak and unlike so many evangelists of his day he was sincere. You felt the message was being given to you personally. His premise was we have all sinned and fallen away from God causing God to send his "only begotten son" Jesus to die on the cross as payment for our sins. We could only be saved if we turned our life over to Jesus. "For all have sinned and come short of the glory of God," Billy Graham quoted from the Bible.

According to Billy Graham God has a plan for your life, a good plan, and if you believe in Jesus and the Bible, walked the straight and narrow you will be open to all the good God has planned for you. I had never heard this part of his message in my church. During the duration of the Crusade I went frequently and on the last night I went forward and gave my life to Christ.

This experience would be the foundation for the cornerstone of my life, but it did not pertain to me. We are all different, but I made an agreement to play this negative role, thus causing me to blame myself when my mental illness did not dissipate. Well meaning, but ignorant Christians told me to exercise my faith, to trust God more.

I did not know on this summer evening when I gave my life to Christ my first full fledge attack of mental illness would not come for several years. I only knew I was not like other people. The anxiety attacks I was experiencing were just the beginning of an illness I would live with the rest of my life. I built my life on the Christian premise and that would compound the problems I would face.

Recently I read Billy Graham's autobiography. His religious education is not impressive. What I found unbelievable was how proud he is of his ability, as a young man, to milk a large number of cows in a short time. This lack of sophistication combined with his good looks and literal translation of the Bible, whose sermons were written by a professional writer, were the components of a man who changed lives, especially my life.

TOM

At sixteen my life began to take on a new dimension. As Billy Graham had preached, "God has someone he has chosen just for you," if you do what God told you. I thought a lot about this. I wanted so much to have a husband to love and please and children to rear. I had not come to terms with this vague uneasiness inside me. I prayed. I attended church. My life revolved around the church.

The man God picked out for me, or so I thought, was the new Intern at our church. His name was Tom. He was twenty-three, over six-feet tall and ordinary looking, but the clerical collar set him apart from other men. The first time he asked me out I felt special and very mature. He was quiet, did not drink, but was a heavy smoker and I considered this very manly. We talked about religion and I noticed he was very legalistic. Everything was black or white, which matched my views. There was only one way to God and we were most certainly on the path.

We were married in the summer of 1959, shortly after Tom had been ordained. The morning of our wedding day Tom was to meet his parents and me in a restaurant at 7:30 a.m. for breakfast. The hours past slowly until noon when Tom arrived. His mother was angry but he said nothing except, "I had to put the boat hitch on the car." I wanted to forget this experience and tried to understand Tom's viewpoint. Words like, "why didn't you call the restaurant?" were never spoken.

The wedding went as planned and we left for our honeymoon We had a comfortable room with a beautiful view of the lake. Then came the time I had saved myself for the man who would be my husband. Both Billy Graham and my mother had stressed the importance of being a virgin. He penetrated me I screamed the scream of intense pain. We tried for several hours. I was in pain. Tom showed no sign of any emotion except disgust. I cried myself to sleep.

The next morning we drove to a doctor's office in silence. The doctor confirmed my worst fears the hymen would have to be broken surgically once we returned home. We still had ten days at the lodge and decided to stay. Tom barely spoke to me during this time. I felt isolated. The abstinence I was told would be required now seemed to be keeping us apart. The honeymoon set the stage for the marriage. He was cold and indifferent. If I had to pick one word to describe our marriage it would be neglect. He lacked a personal life. Instead he was consumed by goals in the parish and the church hierarchy. He proved to be a cold unhappy man. There were rumors about his infidelities. He had a blackboard in his office. At the top of it he wrote, "Goals for the parish." Most of his goals were achieved at the expense of our family.

I felt trapped but I was not alone. A neighboring pastor's wife confided in me that her six-year old son only wanted to play with girls' toys and dress like her. When they took him to a psychiatrist it was discovered her son had no idea how a man was supposed to act because his father was rarely home. When his father took time off he spent it fishing with his brother, also a pastor.

In 1961 we had a son who we named Thomas Michael. Tommy proved to be a delightful child. He was a joy and I loved him so much. His father was gone days, evenings and nights. I was so happy to have Tommy.

THE BETRAYAL

I've heard it said that the clergy are just like any other men. They put the pants on one leg at a time. If only it was that simple. It has been my experience they are not like other men. They are ridden with pride, excusing themselves from all of depraved sexual acts. Tom was no exception.

On my twentieth birthday, we were supposed to see Tom's parents. Seeing his parents had become a ritual on his day off. I told him I wanted to spend the day with him and no one else. Then he said he had something important to tell me. He began, "My psychiatrist told me never to tell my wife this but I must for Mother and Dad's sake. Before I met you I was arrested because of a sex related crime. I was sentenced to three years in Maynard Penitentiary for the criminally insane. Mother, Dad, and the Dean of the Seminary used all their power and I was given probation with the provision I see a psychiatrist. I was supposed to see one in New York, but the pastor to who I reported said it was not necessary." I could feel the disgust as I ran for the bathroom vomiting even before I got there. Who had I married? I thought ministers were supposed to care about people's feelings. Every hope and dream for the marriage had ended.

Today, some forty years later we still see the church protecting sex offenders. The Catholic Church is trying desperately to both cover up the behavior and find some explanation for its Priests.

The Catholic Church is not alone. In the last Lutheran Church I belonged to in Florida the pastor stepped down for womanizing and alcoholism. I left before this incident because I got tired of hearing the pastor preach how women were the cause of every problem. My mental health did not need a tongue lashing each week. There was no comfort here just more about punishment.

The clergy play God and act like the devil. So many of my life decisions were made on the basis of Christianity and the ignorance that accompanies it. I search for most of my life to find meaning for my life within the parameters of religion. In his book, *People of the Lie*, Scott Peck writes, "Where else would evil go to hide, but in the church?"

As my life progressed I would find this to be true of the many people I trusted until I found it necessary to leave the church. The belief that I was evil and not worthy of a healing in God's sight would no longer work. My first real help was not from God but an atheist psychiatrist.

Tom and I were living in a town of one thousand people far from television and radio stations. I was alone most nights. At twelve o'clock midnight the television and radio were off the air. The mice in the house, no longer hearing the noise, came out to play. I was frightened. My anxiety was getting worse. Members of our congregation often gave us liquor as Christmas gifts, but neither of us drank. We stored it above the refrigerator. I thought that if I had something to drink I would relax. I poured the whiskey into a water tumbler and drank it all at once. It tasted terrible. I gagged, but it worked. I was able to sleep.

The next day I asked Tom again to talk to a church trustee about the mice in the house. He did not say anything. After a few minutes I shoved him. He knocked me to the floor and slapped me in the face several times. Then he went up stairs to bed.

The next day an exterminator came. He put poison under the cabinets, so most of the mice would eat it, get thirsty, and go outside the house. It took awhile for the poison to work and in the meantime I had my whiskey to drink at night. While I was able to keep up my duties I was tiring easily, felt sick at times and had lost all interest in eating. I weighed 85 pounds.

We moved to a different parish. At the same time a baby was placed in our family. We had been trying to adopt a foreign child but the agency gave us a blond haired blue eyed baby girl. It was all too much for me. Our daughter, whom we named Kathleen, was a difficult child. She cried most of the time and required a lot of attention.

"I can't do it anymore. I'm too sick," I said. "I have people dying who don't carry on as badly as you do," Tom replied. I sat on a kitchen chair and put my head down and cried. "Please don't do this to me," I said. He walked out of the house. I went to bed.

When Tom came home and saw nothing had been done in the house and I was sleeping he woke me up. He asked about care of the house and dinner. "Nothing," I said in a low voice, "and nothing is going to happen till you get me some help. Where are all the good Christian people? Most of the boxes from the move are unopened. Kathleen needs a lot more attention than Tommy ever did. I don't care what the doctor says, I'm sick." By now I had stopped drinking. This was a new home with no mice.

I went to a doctor at the clinic. The doctor talked to me and concluded I was depressed. He prescribed an anti-depressant. After I was taking it for a week I could sense an improvement. When Tom found out I was taking medicine he threw it away. "Depression is a sin. If you feel depressed pray about it but don't take drugs," he said.

Several days later I began to cry and could not stop. I went back to the same doctor and he was appalled at the sight of me. He put me in the hospital. Tests were taken. The same doctor asked me if I drank a lot of alcohol? I said no. I did not consider my drinking days when I was frightened by the mice. I thought of drinking as something that glamorous people do sitting in a luxurious place, not in their bedrooms swallowing and gagging. This was not drinking. You do drink he said firmly and you have damaged your liver and your kidneys. I told him about the mice. He seemed satisfied. "I'm not going to tell your husband what is wrong with you. I will just tell him you have and infection and need rest. I'm going to prescribe an anti depressant for you again." said the doctor.

In a few days I went home. Tom had found my anti-depression medicine and once again threw it away. He told me he had gone to all four pharmacies in town and told them not to fill any more prescription for antidepressants. My doctor helped me by calling a pharmacy in another town and I was able to get my medicine there. I was very careful to hide it where it would not be discovered.

The only person who knew about my moods was my husband. He was brutal when I was depressed and enjoyed my company when I was manic. However this illness did not always fit his schedule and I found it easier to try to act "normal" but as time wore on it became more difficult, especially since I was not diagnosed.

The depression took on the angry mood of aggravated depression. I would lunge at him and the passive behavior he used to control me. I shoved him but his long arms twisted mine behind me. I kicked and screamed and bit him. Finally I would collapse on the sofa sobbing.

FRAGMENTS 1957–1974

COLLEGE

In the fall of 1968 I enrolled in college. Kathleen was in nursery school until the afternoon and Tommy was in school until 3:00 p.m. It was around the children's schedules that I planned my classes.

In this small college forty minutes away from home I felt safe. I also believed that with a degree I could support my children and leave my husband. In this environment there were no left over Vietnam protesters or signs of Beetle Mania. There were just young middle class American students trying to get an education. At the beginning of my third year I arrived to register, on the wrong day. The man behind the enrollment desk was very nasty. I asked him for classes in the morning and he gave me one at 8:00 a.m. and one at 4:00 p.m. This was not going to work. I pleaded with him, asking him to change my schedule. He handed me my papers and said, "Next."

I gathered up my books and fled to the outside. I leaned against the stone building. My books slid to the ground. I did not know where I was because the campus was a mixture of old and new architecture. I thought I might be in Europe. I have never been to Europe. Tears were running down my face as I tried to think how I would get back to the United States. Suddenly, I saw a familiar face, but I could not remember her name. She was the Lutheran Minister's wife from a nearby town.

She knew I was upset, but I don't believe she knew the extent of my trauma. While we drank coffee and ate jelly donuts she chatted about her own marriage and how difficult life had become. As she talked I remembered I was at school. No one would have to know about this and perhaps I would be safe.

This incident changed my life. I never went back to school again. When I left I had a 3.57 grade-point average and I was member of the Student Advisory Council.

This illustrates how fragile the mind is and illustrates how Attention Deficit Disorder when left unchecked, can create confusion and upset. (At this point in time very few people knew about Attention Deficit Disorder.) However, for me the misreading of a letter became an unexpected detour in my life.

NANCY

Tom insisted I go with him and stay with a family from our congregation in the hospital waiting room. Their teenage daughter, Nancy, had appendicitis and her kidneys were failing. This went on for about five days. Each day the doctor would say he was moving Nancy to Chicago's Michael Reese Hospital and have her placed in the kidney machine. On one of these days Tom insisted I spend time in Nancy's room. I went in, but tried not to look at her. A lot of things did not make sense to me. The doctor stayed at the hospital all day every day. His office was backing up with patients. He was middle aged so this would not be the first time he lost a patient. I saw some of cards on the nightstand in Nancy's room and began to read them. All the cards were typical get well cards except one it read, "Congratulations to you and the little one." She had an abortion! I knew it, and this was the reason the doctor was reluctant to move her even when it was her only chance to survive. Abortions were against the law and the doctor would lose his license.

When we got home I told Tom about the abortion theory and I was surprised when he strongly disagreed with me. I insisted he pressure the doctor to move Nancy to Chicago. Finally Nancy was moved and placed in the kidney machine. My husband and I waited with the family. Her parents went to the chapel and Tom and I talked." She should have been moved days ago," I said. Tom gave me a disgusted look. Nancy's doctor at Michael Reese walked toward us. "She's dead. Who performed the abortion?" he asked.

The hours and the days that followed were one long nightmare. I was elected to pick out the casket. I was twenty years old and did not have the life experience for this task. The floor creaked as we walked into the dimly lit room with caskets. I felt a little faint but I had to hold myself together. Her mother liked one lined in a blue, but it was very expensive. Finally, as I knew it would be, the choice was left to me and I picked a less expensive coffin lined in blue. I could not wait to get out of the room.

The church had an outside sound system prepared for the funeral. Passes were given to family and close friends. No pass was issued to me so I stood outside in the August sun feeling very tired and faint. I was three months pregnant and worried about the baby. We proceeded to the church cemetery. Then the final words, "blessed are the dead who die in the Lord," were spoken. I was just about to get into my car when Nancy's mother asked me to help her arrange the flowers on the grave and come back to her home. I helped with the flowers but declined her offer to go to the house. I was hot and exhausted. As the days passed I was starting to get over the funeral. One evening Nancy's doctor came to our house. He spoke privately with Tom. Two days later he committed suicide.

This was a tragic event and having to participate in these events made me long to be a college student with people that were my own age, and knew freedom and fun. Stress or tragedy does not bring on chemical depression. I was able to be stable and this experience was not followed by a mood swing.

SUICIDE

It was unusually cold in the two story brick home the church provided for us. It was only a few years old and very comfortable. I looked out of the window and saw a sheet of ice covering the street. It was sleeting. I told Tom I would not be making the trip to Champagne, Illinois to pick up Kathleen's glasses. Driving an hour in this weather was too dangerous. I was very depressed and did not want to venture on a long trip.

"You need to get Kathleen's glasses today," his statement caused me to burst into tears. "Don't you care about me," I asked? I went in the living room and sat on the sofa and cried. I had lost all self-control. He brought me my coat and purse. I felt as if I was a robot as I slipped into my coat and then backed the car out of the garage. I was still crying when I got to the main highway. I felt totally worthless, a liability, and also angry with myself for letting him bully me. I was afraid of him. He did not love me and never did. I decided to end my life that day.

It was only a two-lane road and there were plenty of large trucks driving in the opposite lane. I would pull my car in front of one at the very last minute. I felt certain the driver would not be injured and I would die on impact. This would look like an accident and not a suicide. I didn't want the children to have to live the knowledge their mother took her life.

I saw it. The big white truck that would end my life. I waited, waited, NOW! I was close enough to see the driver and then suddenly my car spun around, went off the road and gently slid into a ditch. I was unable to get out. Any motion might make the car tip over. There was not a mark on me, but somehow I felt defeated.

A Highway Patrol car pulled onto the side of the road. "Are you all right?" asked the officer. I responded, "yes". He instructed me to try not to move around because the car could tip. "I'm going to take you out through the window," he said. I took my coat off to make it easier, and with his help I was out of the car!

The officer gave me a ride home. I'll talk to your husband," he said. The officer was a large man and I was standing behind him when Tom answered the door. "What happened to my car?" he asked. The officer became very angry.

"Don't you want to know about your wife? Tom was aggravated. "Just tell me about the car," he said once more.

The car had to be towed out of the ditch but there was nothing wrong with it. I laid on the bed crying about the many people who die each year in accidents. These people were leading a productive life and a happy life. I wish for death and it would not claim me.

I am convinced quality of life comes from physical and mental well being. This episode took place when I was twenty-seven. There was no lithium or many of the new medicines we have today. You rode out your moods. If I had been in a normal state of mind I would not have gone. If my depression had taken the form of aggravated depression I might have argued with him and become verbally abusive and I would not have gone. If I were in a manic state I might experience the world as a winter wonderland and eagerly undertaken the trip. Perhaps I might then also do some shopping.

Not every one is like me as far as length of moods. I rapid cycle so my mood s change quickly. This enabled me to stay in the work force. Some people experience the same mood for months or even years. You can't choose your moods. They visit you at their convenience.

CHRISTMAS

It was just after Thanksgiving, and as we drove along the country roads there was nothing to look at but miles of flat barren land where a few short weeks before a crop of tall corn had stood. I found the fields depressing and my mission to accompany my husband to the church Circuit Conference even more so. There were eleven pastors and their wives in attendance. The wives met separately and discussed their children, recipes and their husbands in such a manner to lead one to believe on judgement day their husband would certainly be seated on the right hand of God. I usually did not say much, but carefully looked at my watch hoping the time would come when I could go home. I felt like crying this morning and begged Tom to let me stay home, but he told me I was expected to attend. He made it sound as if staying home were breaking a commandment. So I went.

The women began to talk about Christmas decorating, baking, and the many extra duties we as pastor's wives had at this time. I began to feel very guilty because I felt this year I would not be able to function at the level expected. I often wrote the Children's Christmas Program and I knew the feelings of joy and merriment could not to be found in me. As I listened to talk about homemade candy, homemade candles, personalized gifts for friends, Christmas trees in each of the children's rooms, and as one woman put it all it, "Christmas all through the house," I began feeling guilty and even more depressed.

I always finished my Christmas shopping by the end of October. I knew if I was at a low functioning level at Christmas time the children would have gifts. We had an extra bedroom and I wrapped the gifts and hid them here. I had the 250 Christmas cards ready to be sent by December on a nightstand. All I had to do is remember to mail them.

There were small things I did for the children. We had an Advent Wreath and the children took turns lighting and extinguishing the purple candles. I tried to have a small gift for them at the beginning of each week in Advent, but I doubted I would this year. It seemed impossible to collect my thoughts or make any decision.

Decorating the tree was always a hassle. I tried to make it nice by serving hot chocolate and cookies. This year the cookies were not homemade. Tom was a perfectionist and the children had their own way of doing things. It wasn't always a happy experience.

I thought about the woman who had Christmas all through the house and I felt like a failure. I went up to my bedroom and fell asleep.

NEW ORLEANS

I woke up to find myself wrapped in blankets on the floor of a seedy motel bathroom. The roaches were crawling up and down the walls and I was confused. Slowly the events of the last ten days were coming back to me. I had wanted to go to New Orleans for New Year's and convinced Tom and another couple it would be a blast. It took some convincing especially when we tried to make reservations for rooms. The Sugar Bowl was being held in New Orleans. Not to be stopped by such a minor detail I called a friend who lived in the area and she had arranged for this motel.

On the way to New Orleans I was very chatty and had an abundance of energy, which is not the best thing in a car. When we arrived at the hotel I was angry and disgusted. How could my friend make reservations in such a dump? I insisted we go back to St. Louis and celebrate the New Year there. No one paid any attention to me and they brought the luggage into the motel. It was cold in New Orleans and the room had no heat.

As I dressed for dinner and a night out I calmed down. We were here to have fun. We had dinner at a well-known restaurant and then made the rounds of the clubs and shops. It was not as glamorous as I expected, but at least I could experience a New Year's Eve in the French Quarter. During the course of the day I could feel some of my enthusiasm draining away and I began to feel like crying. I was not going to spoil it for everyone. By midnight I was fighting back the tears and I realized I should not have let my husband take my medicine away again.

We got into bed and I was shaking and crying. I was afraid I would wake Tom and there would be a scene. I took one blanket and my pillow from the bed and slept on the bathroom floor. I slept most of the way home.

An experience that could have been wonderful turned into a nightmare. I slept for several days. Once I was home I arranged with my doctor to get the antidepressant again.

BROWN COUNTY, INDIANA

(From my October 1968 journal) I'm tired and cold so I won't write much. I can't believe today really happened. Ed, his wife, and their two boys came over. Our plans were to go to Brown County and see the foliage and then visit Nashville, Indiana with it many shops.

Ed and I got into a disagreement about the type of vestments Martin Luther wore. It escalated and I ended the conversation by saying, "Don't trust anyone over thirty." Ed really got mad. He, like all the other adults, was over thirty. We left for Brown County in rain and the rain continued. Ed was driving and once inside a state park Ed stopped the station wagon and said, "every adult under thirty get out." That meant me.

I opened the door and got out. My shoes were taking on water, my hair was soaking wet and the rain was cold. Tom got out of the wagon and tried to drag me inside. I kicked him in the shins and began running to an area the wagon would not be able to enter. I sat down on a picnic bench and tried to think how I would get home. I decided it would be best to walk the five miles to Nashville.

I can't remember when I felt so cold, but it also was kind of an adventure, a game. I was in a manic state. My clothes were soaked and my hair clung to my face. Hours later I arrived in Nashville and saw my answer to a way home. It was a tour bus and the sign read, "Danville," which was just one half hour from home. I approached the driver and asked him if he could take me back to Danville with his tour. He said he had room, but his tour didn't leave for two more hours. I let him know it was fine with me. I decided to wait in the bus, but after awhile the wet clothing was making me so cold. I realized what I would look like when I arrived in Danville, so I left the bus and used my credit card to buy a blue sweater, a jean skirt and some navy loafers. It felt so good to be in dry clothes. The next step was to have my hair washed and dried.

The bus ride home was very long and even longer for me as I anticipated my reception from Tom. Finally we arrived in Danville. I called Tom from the bus station. He was surprised to learn I was in Danville. He said he would be there soon. He arrived with two sheriff's deputies. I was glad I had bought the new clothes and had my hair dried in Nashville. I greeted the deputies first with a big smile. I told them it has really been a crazy day. I acted very relaxed and kissed my husband on the cheek, then smiled at the officers. I told them Tom worries about me so much. I did get separated from my party, but everything turned out just fine. The officers looked at each other and left. If I had not bought those clothes and had my hair done I would be spending tonight in a mental hospital.

AVON

Just before Tommy celebrated his eight birthday he asked me if we were poor. His friends had color televisions and had been to Disneyland, but we didn't seem to be able to do or have what other people did. I assured Tommy we weren't poor, however his friends' families did have more income than we did.

I had been thinking of getting a part-time job, but I was concerned about my mood swings. When I read the ad for Avon I knew this would work for me. I could be home when the children arrived home from school and not work on days I was depressed.

I started on January 3rd. Most potential customers were still facing the reality of Christmas bills and it was snowing. I began to question my decision. I went door to door in my assigned territory. Most of the people invited me in. Some made purchases, but most did not. It would have been easy to become discouraged, but my mood was stable and I continued. I kept calling on people in my territory and after two weeks I sent in an order for $187.00. Forty percent of that would be my profit.

Each month my sales grew. I was made a member of the President's Club, which gave me special discounts. My manager was very pleased. Most of my clients looked forward to seeing me. I realized the women who worked during the day were being overlooked. I took Kathleen, who was then four years old, with me. She behaved and many of these women had special treats for her. There was a bonus to taking Kathleen with me, as Avon perfumes and her body chemistry worked great together. If I took Kathleen, she would wear the perfume and there were more perfume sales. The money I earned was used to take the children to Disney World and other attractions in Florida. We bought two color televisions and there was money for small luxuries.

Several years later Tom asked me for $2000. He wanted to leave the ministry, and there was a firm in Chicago working with ministers and priests who wanted to find positions outside the church. I gave it to him because I believed he wanted to change and have time for me and the children. This was not the case.

HIGH MOODS

During my manic moods the children and I used to have moments of laughter and fun, sometimes at my expense. When every thing seemed like a joke to me the children participated and there was laughter. On one such occasion we had eight people coming to dinner at our house. The guests were slowly arriving and the turkey needed to be checked. As I opened the oven door I slipped on some grease. While I was ok my wig went flying and landed on the turkey's breast. The three of us started laughing. Tom came in wearing his usual frown and said get that thing off the turkey before someone comes back here. H e picked the wig off the turkey and said, "here do what you do with these things." Tommy and Kathleen could not stop laughing. As a joke I put the wig on and turkey juice came running down my face and neck. We started laughing again. Tom was back. "What's going on here," he said. "I'm just doing what you said. I'm wearing the wig because you told me to." "Do you realize you have eight people waiting for dinner," he asked?" "Oh," I said, "just ask them with or without the wig."

On another occasion we were driving into the country. I often took the children to Rock Home Gardens. It was an hour's drive, deep into the Amish Country. The gardens were beautiful and encompassing everything one could want in the outdoors. The flower gardens were a splendid palette of colors and greenery. The children loved the playhouses, some which were high in trees and others on the ground. We ate a picnic lunch and then went back to what pleased us the most. In my case it was the gardens. Sprinkled through out the garden were plaques with Amish sayings. The one that always made me laugh was, "Kissin' don't last, cookin' do."

On one such occasion, shortly before we reached the park I saw an auction in progress and an old storage trunk I wanted. I pulled the car over to the side, jumped out and told the children to stay in the car. I ran to the gate, got a number, but the trunk was sold. Oblivious to all around me I located the new owner. "Would you like to double your money?" I asked. "Believe I would," he said. I paid him and picked up the trunk and happily put the trunk in the car.

When I got behind the steering wheel the children were laughing. "Look at the auction," said Tommy. I could not believe I could have just crashed an Amish auction wearing my tee shirt and shorts. The women and men all were dressed in black clothing that covered most of their body.

This is Attention Deficit Disorder...***Impulsive!***

See the auction
Run to the auction
Notice nothing but the trunk
Get the trunk
Get the message after the fact

DICK

The years of abuse brought on by my fourteen-year marriage to Tom are best described as neglect. We saw four movies in our fourteen years of marriage. He took a day off every two weeks and we spent it with his parents. Tom and his father would leave Tommy and me with his mother and grandmother, who insisted upon talking about morbid experiences from the past.

On a normal day I would see him at about noon for an hour while we ate lunch together. He returned home at 5:30 p.m. and we would have dinner with the children. He left home at 6:30 p.m. When he came home at around midnight I was asleep.

It was from this void of love and acceptance that I felt this need to be loved and accepted. Dick was a Trustee in our church and I came to know him very well. He felt neglected by his wife and needed someone to stabilize his life. After knowing him for many years I felt he loved me and I could return his love. His marriage had been over long before I met him. He was just going through the motions as I was doing. Through a series of incidents we came together to express our feelings and most of all our need to have someone for companionship and love.

I never thought of the consequences of the affair. I just felt loved. It was wonderful to feel loved and needed. I had more of a life with Dick than I did with Tom. When Tom did find out he divorced me. The same day the divorce was final he married his secretary.

A year after my divorce Dick and I moved to Florida with my children. We were married. I had never been happier in my live. I found a job and Dick began to look for work. By the time we were married a year he had held eight jobs.

This produced a continuous feeling of upset in my life. I continued to work, although this was never the plan. It was very difficult to go to work when I felt depressed and some days I had to stay home or I would cry on my way to work. The determination to do this came because it was necessary to keep the children with me.

Dick is an arrested alcoholic. I have Bipolar Mood Disorder and Attention Deficit Disorder. Dick drank sixteen cups of coffee a day, and coffee is another drug. I have learned from my psychiatrist **people with mood disorders are attracted to people with mood disorders**. There is an inner knowing which attracts these individuals to each other. You recognize something, usually pain, in the other person that draws you toward them. If you find yourself in this situation I advise you move on.

FRAGMENTS 1974–1985

FLORENCE LITTLE

Florence Little was a psychiatric nurse who did some private counseling. I first met her at a church where she was teaching transactional analysis classes. In one of her classes she mentioned that her father and son both had committed suicide, and that she felt if they had been taught transactional analysis they would still be alive. She made a convincing argument for using transactional analysis.

Florence taught individual classes too. I was hoping she could help me. Our meetings were never on the same time or day. She would call me when she was ready and we would set up an appointment. When six weeks went by and she did not call and I was starting the downward spiral into depression I called her. Florence's husband answered the phone. I was shocked when he told me Florence had committed suicide.

Courses like transactional analysis and other self-help courses are designed for people not suffering from mood-related illnesses and a runaway brain. It is hard not to grasp for straws when you get on your own nerves and then in desperation it becomes tempting to look outside the medical profession for help. My experience as a searcher tells me your help lies in finding the right medication for you.

Herbs are something that has been around forever and have suddenly become the **new** wonder drug for some people. Speaking from my intense experience ten years ago with a herbalist **they do not work!** My herbalist mixed these concoctions and gave me a schedule to follow. In a matter of days I was bedridden and severely depressed. I thought of killing myself. You can do as I did and look to the church, holistic medicine, self-help books, or herbalists, but I have found the only answer to be a good psychiatrist and the right medicine.

Here is an example to consider. A man has a bad heart condition. Would you take him to church to get well? Would you hand him a self-help book? Would you take him to a herbalist? You would more than likely take him to a heart specialist who would prescribe the appropriate medicine.

The mentally ill have been made to feel guilty about their need for medicine. This is where positive attitude nonsense comes into play. I never knew anyone who won the lottery because he had a positive attitude, but I know a lot of people who had a positive attitude about winning the lottery and did **not** win it.

I recently came across a very old copy of *The Power of Positive Thinking*, by Norman Vincent Peale, pastor of the large and prestigious Marble Collegiate Church in New York. I was surprised to find in his earlier version of the book he asserted that people who suffer from mental illness are weak people and positive thinking was a must for them. Once again, a representative of the church strikes out against the mentally ill. Church people are still quoting Peale's sentiments. It comes from the belief that the mentally ill are being punished by God and therefore people should not try to help the mentally ill because it would be going against "God's will." You must first get a positive attitude.

So many times I have heard "What's the matter with you?" "Look on the bright side." "Get a positive attitude." What world do these people live in? Would World War II have been different if we told the Jewish people in concentration camps to have a positive attitude?

GLENDA COX

Glenda Cox was my first in a long list of psychologists. She was in her early fifties, short with dark hair and she definitely dressed for comfort. When we sat down I could see her stocking rolled just below her knee and her clothes fit loosely, almost as if they were a size too big.

She hugged me when I came into the church and showed me to her office. She indicated it would be best if I talked to Jesus first and then I could talk to her. She placed an empty chair in front of me and told me to talk to Jesus. "Just pretend he is in sitting here, dear, and talk."

I told Jesus my problems. She would interject by telling me to continue or sit up straight. I was in one of my depressed moods so it was just easier to go along and not question anything.

I continued to see Glenda and over a period of two months she had me wean myself off my medicine for depression. I told her I was afraid my mood would elevate and she assured me Jesus would protect me.

After I was totally off my medicine for three weeks I began to feel very good. I had a wonderful life ahead of me. I had extra energy now so I used it to go to the mall and shop. I actually believed Jesus, who had brought about this healing, about would see that the charges were paid.

One Saturday I went to a fast food chicken place to pick up lunch for the family. I was going out the exit drive when a woman drove in the wrong way. All I would have to do was back up a car length and she could pass. I was so manic I would not move my car. The other car was blocking part of a major intersection. Cars were everywhere. I just sat in my car feeling such a determination to hold my position and not give in. Horns began to blow and there was utter chaos in the streets. A police car pulled up and I was surprised when the officer walked toward my car. I had done nothing wrong. He asked me to move my car. The same manic driving force within me led me to tell him, "No."

"You have the whole northeast section of St. Petersburg in a grid lock." he said. "She is the one who drove into the driveway against the arrow," I replied. The officer had his citation book out. I told him I had committed no violation.

"I'm going to write you up for failing to obey a police officer." I moved my car and after an hour traffic finally cleared.

A few days later I was no longer driven by this manic state. I woke up crying and could not stop. I was unable to go to work. Usually this pattern would last a day or two but this time I was in bed crying for six weeks. I resumed taking my medicine and eventually was able to return to work.

After years of searching I have come to the conclusion we have a path to walk to move our soul along. It is not the function of Jesus, Buddha, Yoganada, or other highly evolved souls or avatars to intervene in the experiences we have chosen for this lifetime. When Jesus was in the garden, before his crucifixion, he prayed, "Father if there is anyway let this cup be removed from me." He is talking here of an experience which he chose to move his soul along, but his prayer did not change the circumstances. He was put to death.

Think long and hard before you introduce a religious belief that does not leave room for your illness. If you are mentally ill, you are not being punished, and you are not a bad person. Do not allow any religion to convince you your medicines are not necessary because you have reached an exalted state of grace. Ignorant people sit the closest to the godhead. Don't let them ruin your life.

I JOINED THE RESERVES (ALMOST)

Dick and I constantly had financial problems, especially when we wanted a few luxuries. We had thought of selling merchandise at the Flea Market but we had no connections with a wholesaler that would allow us to purchase goods to resell. It would also mean giving up our weekends. Someone I worked with was in a similar situation, but one afternoon she announced the answer to her problem. She was joining the Reserves. It was only two weekends a month and you received benefits, too. When lunchtime came I went to see the recruiter. It was true, work two weekends a month and I could buy a van, more trips to Disney World, new furniture, a swimming pool, and maybe a trip to Europe.

When Dick came home that evening he was not pleased to hear about my decision to join the Reserves. That did not stop me because I knew I could do it. In fact, I thought it would be fun. I was so excited in this manic mood that I asked everyone to sit down in the dinning room and vote on whether to get a van or a swimming pool first. The children were excited. They both picked the van.

Kathleen asked me if she had to salute me once I joined the service. "No," I said, "just Dick will have to salute because he was in the army." Dick was not amused. He came back in the room and asked me, "Who is going to call in sick for you the first time you can't get out of bed on a Reserve day?" "I don't think there will be anymore black days," I said. "It will be good for me. I'll learn self-discipline and then I will control myself a lot better. "Get your head out of your ass," he said. "This has nothing to do with self-discipline. Your mood swings continue to upset everyone. Now the kids think we are getting a van. They're calling all their friends and telling them. You know what? You are as crazy as a shit house rat."

In a few days my manic mood passed. I tried to explain what happened to the children but the pain of not getting a van made them angry with me. I never applied to join the Reserves. In a normal state I knew I could not control my moods in the future.

DESPAIR AND THE CHURCH

I've experienced physical pain having had two major operations, and giving birth, but the pain cause by mental illness is different. It permeates the soul. It makes you beg God for mercy and then curse Him when relief does not come.

Depression is a soup kettle made up of abandonment, anger, mood swings and the wish for death. Physical pain is sharp but there is the hope for healing. Medicine is given to relieve the pain and there are friends and family for support.

The church through the ages has made depression and it partner despair a sin. Thirty years ago it was consider a sin to see a psychiatrist. Today, we are told to pray about our depression, the ask for forgiveness for whatever we did to bring the depression about, look on the bright side, and to have a positive attitude. The ignorance abounds.

The mentally ill are bombarded by the voices of the cruel and uninformed. Most people who are not mentally ill cannot comprehend the pain and despair which comes with depression. They feel they are stronger, thinking God is punishing the mentally ill. They view the mentally ill as cowards and feel that mental illness is a composite of a weak faith and lack of character.

Unlike other illnesses, there is usually no understanding of the illness even by the family members.

There are good books available to educate people, and they are not all written by psychiatrists. People who have the illness have written many informative books. As you experience their pain there is room for understanding.

Until understanding is created between family members and the mentally ill, life will be difficult for all involved. Instead of helping the mentally ill some families keep waiting for the day when the manic depressive will get his act together, thereby denying the illness and causing pain for themselves. There are places for families to go. One place is the local chapter of the National Alliance for the Mentally Ill.

COURT CLERK

I had been working at the Courthouse for about five years when I was offered the position of Court Clerk. This position would take me a way from the front counter and supervisory duties. Unfortunately for me, this was one of my "flying high" days. I was out going and felt I was up to any challenge. The truth is at this moment I was feeling excited and happy.

The fact is I lacked many of the qualities this job required. I had to sit in one place in the courtroom and take depositions. It was often rapid fire and easy to miss part of a deposition. The defendants would often try to ask me questions and while I was trying to address these questions I would miss part of the deposition. Sometime the bailiff would help me, but his function was to protect the judge, not act as my back up.

And then it happened. It was a day I will never forget. When I was taking the dockets out of the copy machine I dropped them. Each docket had about six pages and eighteen different people had to get copies. I picked them up, grabbed the stapler, but there were no staples. I succeeded in getting a stapler when the bailiff came and told me the judge was going to start without me. "Just give me two dockets," he said. I put a third docket together for myself. Once in the courtroom the judge was hearing the case of a man who had multiple fines and had not paid any of them. The judge read the fine amounts and then turned to me and asked me for the total. "Could you give the fines to me one more time?" I asked. He did. Every time I added the numbers they were different. I knew the Judge was getting annoyed. "Well Madam Clerk, What is the sum total of all the fines?"

This day, as others to come, would give testimony to the marriage of manic depression and Attention Deficit Disorder (ADD), the dynamic duo. These unwanted guests in my life had once again left me humiliated.

My Explanation:

My acceptance of the position came from the impulsiveness of ADD mixed with a manic depression, manic stat

The dropping the dockets came from ADD caused lack of hand/eye co-ordination

Not being able to add the fines came from ADD caused learning disability in math

Being overwhelmed came from a manic depression, depressed state

TACO BELL KITCHEN

It was 1977 and I was having lunch at Taco Bell with a co-worker. The beauty of this fast-food restaurant had me spellbound. The walls were done in a soft sand color and bricks were evenly imbedded in the wall. I felt as if I was in Mexico. I was enchanted by everything from the red plastic trays to the lighting.

I told my co-worker I thought I would redo my kitchen to resemble Taco Bell. She laughed and we went back to work. I spent the afternoon mentally planning my Taco Bell kitchen. At dinner I announced, with great enthusiasm, my plans to redo the kitchen so it would look like a Taco Bell. No one paid any attention to me. However, in the next week I gather the necessary supplies to turn my kitchen into a work of great beauty. Dick, who until this point thought this was one of my mood swings and that it should have past by now.

He did not realize the magnitude of the problem. He tried reasoning with me but I interrupted him by describing the beautiful kitchen we would have. He began to think that perhaps this was not a mood swing, but that it was actually a rational decorating idea. He waited another week because I rapid cycle. He was convinced my mood would have changed by now. He started work in the kitchen believing this was not a mood swing but the normal behavior of a wife with poor decorating taste.

The kitchen was done. It was splendid. I showed my neighbors and friends who were strangely quiet. I guessed they were as awestruck as I was by its beauty. My children, on the other hand, had plenty to say. Words like disgusting and ugly were used to describe my beautiful Taco Bell kitchen.

After several weeks past, one morning I went into the kitchen and saw that it looked awful. I wondered what had happened to turn my kitchen into a stucco prison. I leaned against the wall and surveyed the room. How could I have let this happen? This was my idea? Dick entered the kitchen. "Beautiful, isn't it?" he said. I could not hold back the tears. I went to bed realizing, once again, that my mind had brought about great pain in my life. The following weekend Dick and I sanded the walls and recovered them with wallpaper. It was a hard task. We worked in silence.

HYSTERECTOMY

I was not unhappy when Dr. Anderson informed me it was time to perform a hysterectomy. I had suffered with endometriosis for most of my adult life. Now, at age thirty-nine, it was a relief to be over the pain and symptoms once the operation was performed.

I was not taking Lithium at this time, but I was taking the same antidepressant prescribed for me when I was twenty-three. Dr. Anderson was adamant that I was to take no medication the day before surgery and while I was in the hospital.

The day of the surgery I remember some pain, but for the most part I slept. Several days later I was discharged along with all my flowers. On the way home I became obsessed with the idea of writing thank you notes. I had to write them **now!**

Dick had taken the week off from work to help me. Once home I discovered I was in a lot more pain than I realized. I gladly stayed in bed and slept. Several hours later I heard Dick cooking in the kitchen and I wondered if I could get passed him and drive to the grocery store to buy some thank you notes. This was despite the doctor's instructions not to drive for the next two weeks. I put on a baggy dress and went to the dining room to get my purse. I tried to lift it and I felt a sharp pain. I thought of going back to bed but I had to get those thank you notes, **now!** I took some money out of my purse, and shoved it in my pocket.

Getting into the car was something I hadn't thought about. I could not open the door. When I saw a boy riding his bike I called to him and he opened the door for me. I gave him a dollar and he was on his way. I was not on my way. The pain I felt as I stepped on the brake was sharp and piercing. I continued. I had to get the thank you notes. Once inside the supermarket I felt light-headed. I went to the card section, but before I could pick out a card I was losing the battle to stay on my feet. I felt myself sway and saw Dick come around the corner. He caught me as I slumped to the floor. We went home without any thank you notes. I was put to bed and Dick called the doctor.

Some people with mental illness can become obsessed with the need to do something. This type of obsession was portrayed by the Melvin Udall character in the movie *As Good As It Gets*. This was an isolated incident for me, probably brought on by missing my medications. However it is driven behavior brought on by a manic state, and in such a state nothing will stand in your way toward accomplishing your goal.

DR. WILLIS

As I approached my fortieth birthday I realized I must see a psychiatrist if I were to continue working and have my children live with me. I spoke to Dick and asked him for help. He agreed I needed to be seen by a doctor and contacted the University of South Florida's Medical Center.

The first time I met Dr. Willis he pleasantly surprised me with his concern and warmth. I was expecting some Sigmund Freud type who would speak with a heavy accent. Dr. Willis spent two hours with me exploring my family history. My grandparents on my father's side were either cousins or brother and sister. They had six children. My father was the youngest. All of the children were mentally ill except the twins. One of the daughters was a Catholic nun. She committed suicide. Most of my father's siblings went on to have children and some of them were and are afflicted.

My mother's parents were both born in Germany but there was no bloodline connection. Their oldest child, a boy, seemed normal to me. He had attained an education beyond high school and became an engineer. He did not smoke or drink. As the oldest child he had to make a decision when his father died at age fifty, to go on with his education or stay and help my grandmother support the three younger children. He left. The second child, a girl, dropped out of high school and became a bookkeeper to help support the family and my grandmother went to work as a cook for a wealthy family.

The third child, a boy of about eleven at the time of his father's death, was a wild boy. He was routinely stealing cars and getting into trouble with the police. However, this was the age of "boys will be boys." He was never detained.

He married young, and fathered two daughters. When the girls were young he started a very successful sewing machine repair business in New York City. He fell in love with a beautiful Italian woman and abandoned his wife and two little girls. He moved to Maine, divorced his first wife, and married the Italian woman. They had three children. He was well on his way to becoming an alcoholic. He continued his drinking, amassing an unbelievable amount of driving while intoxicated violations. Everyone in my family liked him and found him amusing and always willing to help them out.

My mother was the youngest child. It was difficult for me to talk to Dr. Willis about her. My mother and I never got along. When I was younger I thought the problems were my entire fault, because she told me they were. She had two faces. One face was for the immediate family and the other face for the rest of the world.

She wanted to please everyone outside the immediate family. She could be a loving and caring person. If any neighbor was sick she brought them homemade soup. She showed other people a kind side we never saw. She had a sense of humor with others and she agreed with everyone. Alone with my father, brother, and me she was critical and spiteful and prone to violence. She was suspicious of everyone. Her biggest need was to get even with people she felt had wronged her and most of this was played out in our family. If my mother was angry with my father she would tell him she was going to a neighbor's house for ten minutes and stay away for two hours, knowingly causing him to experience separation anxiety.

Dr Willis took notes rapidly. He jotted down the medicines I was taking, and gave me release forms to give to all doctors I had seen in the last ten years. When all the information was returned to him and he had seen me in both a high (manic) and low (depressed) state the information would confirm his belief that I was suffering from manic depression.

He did see me in a manic mood. I found everything funny. He did not and sent me home. A few weeks later I called him crying and unable to cope with life. He told me to see him immediately. I drove across the bridge to Tampa feeling as if it I would never be well. I knew I could never work in this condition.

Dr. Willis was very kind and observant. He asked me many questions. "I'm going to start you on Lithium and see if we can't reduce the intensity of the moods or do away with them completely," he said.

DR. WILLIS AND THE DIAGNOSIS

The first week I took Lithium I became very nauseous. I called Dr. Williams and he thought it was the flu. He instructed me to stay on the Lithium and I did as I was told. By the middle of the second week I felt so sick I started vomiting, but afterwards I felt fine. I waited a few days and there were no "flu" symptoms. I went back on the Lithium and became ill again. I called Doctor Willis and he scheduled an appointment for the following day.

When we met he explained to me there is very little margin for error between a toxic and non-toxic dosage of lithium. He would lower my dosage of Lithium and we would see if it made a difference. I protested, "Isn't there anything else I can take?" "Give it a time, Carol, it's your best chance," he said. I agreed reluctantly.

With the lower dosage I was no longer sick. However, I still waited for my next "high" or "low." Neither one came. I began to wonder about my life. Would it be possible to make plans in advance, with the expectation of a stable mood? As time past I actually had hope that would be the case. It took months before I totally stabilized. I was a new person.

Several months after I started taking Lithium I was getting ready for bed and I saw a strange man in my bedroom. In a split second I saw Dick and then the stranger in the same place. I was very frightened. I slept beside a stranger.

The next morning I called Dr. Willis and told him about this experience. Once in his office he explained while Lithium had stabilized me I was beginning to focus on reality. One man represented the person I created and one was the real Dick. In a rational state you would never have married Dick. This is a psychotic experience. "What happens now," I asked. We work on your marriage and other areas of your life and try to bring your life into focus," was Dr. Willis' response.

I had gone five years without a hint of manic depression. Dr. Willis was seeing me less. When he did see me he talked about the need to address my marriage and my job. We tried counseling with Dr. Willis, but Dick would talk about the weather, the ball games, and the news. Dick was going from one job, to sitting around the house, to finding another job, and back home again. One year he had six jobs.

Dr. Willis continued to ask me why I did not divorce Dick. I told him it was because of the saying, "All the rats leave a sinking ship." "What happens if they don't?" he asked.

Our divorce was peaceful. We sold the house and divided up the contents without incident. My children were in college and graduate school. I had obtained a Florida Real Estate license and went to work for a marketing company specializing in waterfront condominiums. The condominiums were all in some form of litigation and the interest rate was 16%, but most of my buyers were cash buyer looking for an investment. I loved this job.

FRAGMENTS
1985–Present

HONG KONG

It was one of those days when I knew the gods must have been smiling on me. A few minutes after our real estate staff had learned the project had been turn over to another company and that we had no jobs, the phone rang and it was for me.

It was William, the Chinese man I had met on a plane a few months ago. "Can you come work in my business?" he said. "I need you. I never forgot you from the plane," he said. I could not think, but I knew I would be going to work for him. This was a manic person's dream. I gave him my home phone number.

I remembered our first encounter on the plane with pleasure. I was one of the last people to board the plane to New Jersey and was struggling with my coat when William came to my rescue. I'll never forget his words, calling me "My dream woman." We chattered like ancient lovers lost in a time capsule. Each of us refusing our meal for fear it would take from the precious time we had found together.

Once the plane landed we exchanged business cards and parted. I met my son and we drove to my brother's house, which was our destination. We stayed for the weekend and I returned to Florida.

William called and explained his plan. "You will work between Hong Kong and New York with most of your time spent in Hong Kong. I want you to find a boutique item of clothing which will compliment the silk blouses I have in the showroom."

I put my furniture in storage, took care of my financial matters, and went to New Jersey the next week. I stayed with my brother. It was an easy trip by bus from his house to Manhattan.

I worked in the showroom learning procedures as well as practicing eating with chop sticks and learning nine different phrases in Cantonese. I was instructed in proper etiquette. Never refuse food someone offers you, but be very thankful and humble. Do not ask many questions in social situations. William told me he would be in Hong Kong the first few weeks to help me. If he put his finger on his cheek that would mean 'save face' and I needed to check my manners.

We arrived in Hong Kong and were greeted by some of William's family. They seemed very nice, however none of them spoke English. The first place we went was to the New Territories to eat. I needed to use a restroom. I was escorted back to a flimsy curtain, not five feet from where someone was eating. There was a hole in the floor. To make matters worse I had a jumpsuit on and had to get completely out of it, and in doing so watched as my gold pin slip away into the hole. It was hot, I had been on a plane forever, and now I lost my pin. William must have sensed my mood because he gave me the 'save face' sign.

We arrived at the Holiday Inn and got situated in our suite. It was a beautiful suite with elegant wood furniture. William soon presented an interesting problem for me. He was wearing clothes meant for a teenage boy, and when he was wearing them his behavior was brash and argumentative, hardly that of a 60 year old man. He launched most of his attacks at me. I now had to get in the habit of checking his dress to see what kind of a day I was going to experience. Was he sixty or sixteen? I was relieved when he left for New York.

In the next month I found the perfect boutique item. I went to Taiwan to meet with the owner of the factory. We had a good meeting and I arranged for the owner and William to meet. When the meeting took place it was a disaster. I looked at William's clothes and he was wearing clothing a young adult would wear. I began to have suspicions that I was dealing with more than one person. At the same time I was questioning my sanity.

This pattern of changing between personalities based on the clothing William was wearing began to frighten me. I was due to return to New York and I planned to go to Florida and see my psychiatrist. I was getting scared. One night William threw a clock at me because I forgot to send out the laundry. He went so far as to shove me and call me a 'White Ghost,' which is an uncomplimentary Chinese slang term for Caucasians. In between these periods he was a gentleman and I noticed at those times he was wearing a suit. It was becoming too much for me and I could not wait to get back to Florida. I left and after a long uneventful flight I arrived in Florida and took the first appointment my psychiatrist had open. He listened without showing any emotion until I showed him the pictures of William in different attire. He leaned back in his chair and said, as if he were talking to himself, "why do people with mood disorders always fall for people with mood disorders?" He looked through the pictures one more time and suggested I bring this to an end.

I decided to listen to my doctor and not return to either William's or my brother's. My son went to New Jersey and finished up for me. I spent the next six months living with my parent's before I could get over my relationship with one man who belonged to two personalities.

SUSAN SMITH

In a previous fragment I described my disassociation at college. There have been approximately five such incidents in my life.

When Tom, my first husband, died I could not accept the fact that he was not going to come to us some day and apologize for his cruel treatment to me, and especially to my daughter. Suddenly I had this feeling. I knew what to do. I could stop time! It was easy. I got a box and walked through the house with a sense of urgency quickly filling the box with all the clocks in my condominium. I looked at my watch and was frightened because I thought the Salvation Army drop-off center would be closing. I ran for the elevator and drove quickly to the drop-off sight. My heart was racing. I was relieved when I saw they were still open. I dropped off the clocks. A feeling of relief and peace came over me. During the next ten days I would have no recollection of this incident.

Ten days later I found myself looking around the house for a clock. I started opening closet doors because none were in plain sight. Suddenly it all came back to me. It was too much to comprehend to think I could do something so bizarre. When the reality of what I had done hit me I cried for hours wondering if I should even tell anyone. I decided to call my psychiatrist

Another incident occurred when a man I had been dating for three years started to accuse me of seeing another man. I had done nothing to provoke this kind of attack. I remember sitting on the sofa and thinking I should just be still. And then it seemed I disappeared. I was physically on the sofa but I was not there in my mind. I remember nothing of his attack. Time past and I realized I had disassociated, and did not remember anything he said until approximately ten days later. I was in the market and the words he spoke to me that night came back to me, but with the protection of a safe place my mind could respond to the trauma it was unable to accept in the presence of this man. Abuse or an overwhelming experience will cause this type of disassociation.

Several years ago a young mother, Susan Smith, pleaded for the return of her children. She was pathetic as she cried, begging for information about her missing sons. Psychiatrists have told me that the mentally ill have an unconscious way of recognizing each other. I know from my experience I have been attracted to people who are mentally ill and had friendships with them. As I looked at Susan Smith I knew she was mentally ill.

In time the police found Susan Smith's sons at the bottom of a lake. She was shocked and surprised, but she was proven to be the person responsible for their death. I believe some incident made her think her sons would be better off in the lake. It doesn't make sense but neither does putting clocks in a box to stop time.

CHARLES

I had a good job with a placement agency calling on outside accounts while my service coordinator would fill the requests for personnel. I had many friends and raced with the Woman's Yacht Racing Society. I had a very nice life and was in no hurry to get married.

After I was employed at the placement agency for about two years, I woke up one morning crying. I looked in the mirror and it was back. I could not stop crying just as in the past. I called Dr. Willis and he told me to come to his office immediately.

When Dr. Willis saw me he started crying. We sat there both of us crying. Finally I asked, "What am I going to do?" He told me to find the right person and get married. If I didn't have to work I would be okay.

I was dating a man with two Doctorate degrees. He had been married three times. His last wife suffered from manic depression, and according to him he had put her so far away that no one would find the key. On our first date he told me he would never marry again. I was okay with this, because I enjoyed his company and sailing on his large boat. I felt no urgency to marry. I enjoyed being on my own.

This new turn of events caused me to break up with him and join a video dating service. It was through this service that I met Charles. I liked him immediately. Charles was a gentleman, a lover, and friend. I felt protected for the first time in my life. Although he did not look or act seventeen years older than me, the clock would continue to move forward and express itself in our relationship.

I was having problems at work, which I now know now came from Attention Deficit Disorder (ADD). I had been promoted to manager, but declined the promotion because I could not complete the time cards because they needed to be completed using military time. The math learning disability made it impossible for me to learn this system. There was also a problem with the number of sales calls expected. I was required to make four in-person calls a day. Although my dollar ratio was up, the fact was that I could not make more than three sales calls because I kept getting lost when driving. Many people with ADD are said to have no inner compass. I liked this job and the pay was excellent but even making dry runs at night did not help me to find the locations I needed to visit. Shortly thereafter I was let go.

I had to give up my beautiful apartment. I had made arrangements to share an apartment with a woman. Charles came with me the night I signed the lease. I signed it and the leasing agent put it in her basket. Charles took it out and tore it several times. "You're going to live with me," he said kindly.

Living with Charles exposed me to more of his gentle ways. I took a job in advertising sales. I made telephone sales calls and attended conventions in Dallas, Las Vegas, and San Diego. One year we ordered a new style booth for the Las Vegas show. When I practiced putting it up I did not get it right. My manager was very angry. "All I can say is the CEO is going to be there, and you better get it right," she said. The display was shipped to Las Vegas that day.

I was very nervous when I flew to Las Vegas. I checked into the Hilton and then went immediately to the convention center. I looked for my place on the floor. There was a booth like mine already there, and a grinning man standing in the booth. It was Charles. How could you not like this man? He went home that evening.

When I would wake up crying Charles would hold me and put me back in bed. He would call me in sick and stay with me until I fell asleep. He drove all the way from downtown to check on me. He would lie down on the bed with me and hold me for about an hour.

Charles took me to Europe and on cruises, and we always had a wonderful time. I could make Charles laugh. All our conversation was about being together forever.

When Dr Willis left Tampa without telling his patients I became hysterical. Charles saved me from being a permanent resident at a local mental hospital. I was so hysterical I could not stop shaking and forgot how to drive. Charles drove me to the hospital but instructed me not to sign myself in. Once there Charles and I were separated and I signed myself in. I was in the hospital twenty-three hours. I never saw a doctor and was given medicine, prescribed by some unknown person who never even met with me?

I realized almost immediately I had made a mistake. There were only five people on the floor and all were alcoholics. I called Charles and told him I wanted to come home. "I'm working on it," he said.

Fortunately, the next morning I was fine and felt normal when I was interview by the administrator and head nurse. I could see they were surprised by the way I talked and acted, (sometimes it helps to rapid cycle) but they told me I would be staying. I knew Charles would get me out and he did. He never said anything harsh to me, but was very understanding.

I was in the guest bedroom when I heard him say, "I don't care what the procedure is I want the SOB's license pulled. I checked and he's in Jacksonville." The license was pulled. Charles knew many local and national political figures. I was cleaning out a bedroom drawer when I came across pictures of Charles with very high profile people.

After a few years with Charles I noticed a change in him. He was always kind to me but his health was not good and he seemed to talk less. I thought it might be me so I asked him. To my surprise he handed me a bunch of W-2 forms showing his income during the past ten years. He told me he planned to marry me and he wanted me to know he had good earning potential, but as far as everything else it was over. The IRS had audited him and he was in serious trouble. He was going to file for bankruptcy.

I never thought how this might impact me. I loved Charles and wanted to be with him. However, after five years of living together, Charles had a stroke and died soon afterwards. There is so much I could say about Charles as a person. However, it was his help and guidance with my illness I will never forget. He was skilled at being human. He never referred to me as crazy and he understood somewhere inside me was a person worthy of love. He was able to separate the real me from the moods. I have never had this kind of acceptance and love from anyone.

DR. KATZ

Dr. Katz became my psychiatrist after I had tried a number of psychiatrists following Dr. Willis' loss of his license. Dr. Willis was afflicted with manic depression but unable to tolerate Lithium. I don't know what possessed him to leave Tampa without notifying his patients, but I had to get on with my life.

Dr. Katz was a tall, slender man with white hair. He was in his early seventies and had a pleasant calm manner about him. We discussed my medicines. He wanted me to try a new medicine. Some of his patients had improved by using it. It was an anti-seizure medicine. I reminded Dr. Katz I had reverse poles. A person with reverse poles will usually experience the opposite reaction from taking a substance than most other people. For example, while caffeine keeps most people alert, it makes me sleepy. Sleeping pills keep me awake. I was afraid an anti-seizure medicine might make me have a seizure. Dr. Katz assured me this would not happen.

I seemed to be doing well on the medicine. It was a Saturday and I decided to go to the mall. I never even left the parking garage beneath my condominium. I'm not sure what happened but when I became conscious there were paramedics all around me. "You had a seizure," one of the paramedics said. "Do you have epilepsy?" he asked. "No," I said. When I looked at my car the right front and fender had hit the wall and was damaged.

Some of the men pushed the car into a parking spot outside the garage. I went back to my condominium and immediately called Dr. Katz. His answering service reached him quickly. He asked me what kind of insurance I had and I told him it was good. He wanted me to enter a hospital that had a floor for people with depression, alcoholism, and the broad spectrum of mental illness. I could leave any time I wanted he told me. This is not a secure facility. "You can participate in group therapy if you want, or if you don't feel up to it you can stay in your room. This is a pleasant place. I will see you every day."

I decided to go. The facility was much like an expensive hotel. My room overlooked the water. I put my things away and noticed this was not a secure facility. There were no bars on the windows and there was a mirror in the bathroom. It was as Dr. Katz said a place you could leave when you want to.

It was the middle of the afternoon and except for a few people playing pool it was quiet. In thirty minutes people began to move to group therapy. I had a sinking feeling in my stomach. It was obvious that most of the people, about fifteen in number, were experiencing severe emotional pain. If you wanted to speak you were given a chance and sometimes the counselor would ask a question of the group or an individual. These questions were designed to upset you and help you get in touch with your feelings. I thought the counselor was excellent.

I was pleasantly surprised to find the food was excellent, we had our own cook, and there was a beverage for us anytime we wanted it. Most of the women were here for **clinical** depression. This is depression brought on by circumstances and not by a genetic disorder, which results in **chemical** depression. There were a few of us that did fall into the latter category.

My new roommate was like me and suffered from chemical depression. She cried most of the time. She was a pretty young girl, a mother of two, and twenty-three years of age. At first she apologized to me, but I assured her I understood. Then something she said made me very upset. She was here for shock treatments. I left the room and found my counselor. "Stop shaking," he said, "and come in and talk to me." I started to cry. When I was four years old my parents took me to a sanitarium to see me father's sister. She was being wheeled back to her room after shock treatments. She was strapped down, but even that did not stop her from thrashing about. My father was annoyed with my mother and told her to take me outside. It was too late. I will never forget what happened there.

My counselor listened patiently and then explained my roommate would only be given enough voltage to allow her big toe to move. "Things have changed a great deal," he said, "since your aunt had shock treatments. It should help you to know she should feel a lot better." I felt better and decided I could handle it.

The next morning I woke up when the lights were turned on. I looked at my clock. It was 5:00 a.m. and they were moving my roommate onto a stretcher. I turned over and went back to sleep. The next time the lights were turned on she was back. I did not want to look at her. She spoke first. "Carol, I am all right." I turned over and she looked tired but she managed a slight smile and then fell asleep.

The next morning my roommate went to group therapy, but I stayed behind to find out if my car was fixed. I was on an endless hold and then someone came on the line to help me. I had just finished the telephone call and had not slipped into my dress when an orderly entered the room. "Why aren't you at group?" he asked. "I had to call about my car," I said. "You belong in group," he said. I reminded him that group therapy was optional. He was a small man from a third-world country. He moved toward me and I was sure he was going to touch me. I shoved him and he lost his balance and fell backwards. I told him to get out.

I went to group therapy and forgot about the incident, however the head nurse asked me to come to her office. Her first words were "Do you always have trouble with male authority figures?" I was stunned. She was taking his side without hearing from me. "I don't want him near my room again," I said. "That's up to me," she said. "I can always walk out the door and you can explain to Dr. Katz why I am not here." "I'm in charge here, not Dr. Katz," she said. I had just about enough of her. I opened the door to leave and then said, "By the way did you ever hear of patient's rights? The government enforces these rights. Maybe you would like to answer some questions about orderlies walking into patients rooms when they're not dressed." I closed the door hard.

There is no place safe, there is no place you can go or hide, because they brand you as crazy and they have this trump card to play. It's the same card used by family members to exclude you from decisions about yourself.

As I spent the second week in the 'nut house,' as we came to call it, I grew bored and wanted to go home. There was nothing wrong with me. Unfortunately Dr. Katz asked me to wait two more days, causing me to spend my fiftieth birthday in the 'nut house.' It was not a happy birthday. Being fifty is hard enough without having to acknowledge to yourself, once again, you are not like other people.

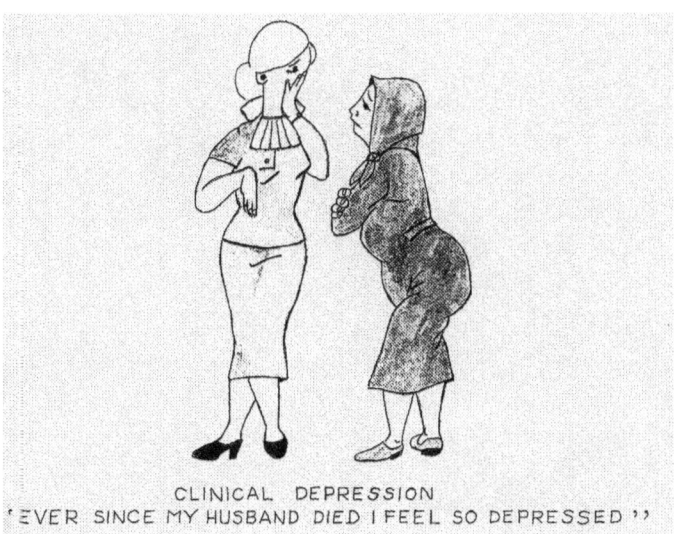

CLINICAL DEPRESSION
"EVER SINCE MY HUSBAND DIED I FEEL SO DEPRESSED"

DAVE

What started out to be an ordinary business phone call with a client quickly changed into casual conversation about how much he liked California and had moved there from the East four years ago when his wife passed away.

He began to call me twice a week and then every day. I noticed he never called me on our toll free line, which showed he had integrity. The toll free lines were not for personal calls. We decided to meet at the next trade show in Dallas. My schedule was already tight but I was hoping something or someone would cancel and give me more time. There was also a large cocktail party. I could make an appearance and then try to leave without being noticed.

The Monday morning the show opened Dave was one of the first people at the booth. He was very attractive, but not in a movie star way .His hair was a sandy color, he had beautiful blue eyes, and his clothing was expensive. I could see my manager looking at me so I had to end the conversation. I told him I would meet him in the main lobby of my hotel at 9:00 p.m.

There was an excellent restaurant in the hotel and we decided to eat there. The wine steward came and Dave asked me what kind of wine I liked. I tried to look very serious and said, "Morgan David." Dave laughed so hard the table was shaking and while the wine steward tried not to laugh, he was smiling. Then I started to laugh and the three of us were all laughing.

We went to a small lounge and had cocktails. David asked me when he would see me again. "I certainly don't want to wait till the next show," he said. He was delighted when I told him I had made plans to see my son in San Diego in a month. "Wonderful, and the next visit will be in Florida," he added.

He held my hand and for a long time and neither of us spoke. I knew David was thinking marriage. We both liked our homes to be comfortable and at the same time beautiful. We shared a love of antiques and art. No one had ever been so right for me. I finally looked at David and asked him what he was thinking about. "Right now I'm thinking you're all I need to complete my world, thus making me the happiest man on the face of the earth," he said. He took my hand and led me to the dance floor. I don't remember the music but the feelings of love and desire will never be forgotten.

The trade show was over and David and I managed one quick goodbye hug. David headed back to San Diego. The first few days back in the office were very hectic. David would call and I would talk for a few minutes. Then it dawned on me I had never given David my home phone number. He sounded relieved when I gave it to him. "Frankly," he said, "I had the feeling you might be living with someone." I laughed. "No, I don't even have a cat or a dog," I said. "That's a relief," Dave said.

The conversations on the phone continued, but I now had two things to worry about. Shouldn't I tell David about my mental condition, and how could I explain tremors in my hands and constantly blinking eyelids. The latter condition was a recent development. I was in great distress, because my clients looked at me as if mesmerized by the eye blinking problem and I could not face David looking like some one out of drug rehabilitation.

The day came for me to fly to my son's in San Diego. I looked in the mirror and hated what I saw. Doctor after doctor told me this was caused by Lithium and there was nothing they could do about it. No beautiful clothes or humorous conversation could make up for the way I looked. With the tremors it was not unusual for me to drop food off my fork. This further distressed me.

My Son picked me up. He was noncommittal about my tremors. David arrived. He was like a child. I hugged him and then sat down keeping my hands out of sight. "Did you get something in your eye?" David asked. He got up and came across the room with his handkerchief in his hand. I told him it would not be necessary. I am under the care of a physician in Florida. "Well you're still beautiful," he said.

We went to the Hotel Del Coronado to eat. I love this place and was so glad David picked it. I don't know that my behavior was up to the hotel's standards. This time when the wine steward came I passed, too afraid wine would make my condition worse. I dropped my fork three times and while trying to pick up my water glass I dropped it and all the water ran towards David who had to jump out of his chair to avoid being soaked. We were just about finished eating. David paid the check and then took me by the elbow. He led me to his car and we both got in. "What is going on here?" he asked. "Do you think I am so stupid. I can see drug abuse? I can't figure out how you managed to keep your self clean for the show. I'm not proud of this, but my oldest son was on drugs and I'll be darned if I will marry someone on drugs."

I told him the 'drugs' I am on are called medicines. "Every one has an excuse, Carol. If I'd marry you I would be another enabler. I made up my mind when I was helping my son I would not do this again." Dave was angry. I knew there was no point in continuing. Dave was like many people who thought the word drug always means harmful. "How many medications do you take?" I snapped at Dave. "None," he said. "I don't even take aspirins." I asked him to take me to my son's. This conversation was futile. David was one of those squeaky clean people who was born with good health and saw the need to take medicine as a character defect. I let myself out of the car, quietly entered the house, and went to bed. The romance was nothing but a dream.

When I went back to work a friend of mine gave me the name of an acupuncture doctor and assured me the doctor could help me. One acupuncture treatment later the tremors and the eye blink problem disappeared. I thought of calling Dave and explaining everything to him. I thought of flying to San Diego and just showing up at his business. I had a responsibility here, too. Dave made it very clear that he liked a peaceful life. It would be very difficult to have one with my mood swings, because even with my medications there were periods of time they just did not hold. In time the pain of what might have been subsided and life went on.

ATTENTION DEFICIT DISORDER

I have not written much about Attention Deficit Disorder and the impact it makes in my daily life and the questions I have about myself. In 1994 a psychiatrist suggested I test for ADD. There are many approaches to diagnose ADD. I spent four days with a psychologist one on one. I learned I had a developmental learning disability in mathematics and was only capable working up to the sixth grade level. I was unable divide numbers correctly. I have no inner compass thus explaining why I was unable to complete only three calls a day at the placement company. I had little hand-eye coordination and my short-term memory was impaired.

Actually, I felt relieved. The test explained my struggle with mathematics most of my life. In high school I was a good student but failed geometry. It explained why I took longer to complete tasks and why I got lost frequently. When I was a child my behavior was Attention Deficit, Depressed. I was not overactive which is usually the reason parent's seek help. There are many subtitled with ADD.

Acting impulsively is the major problem for most people and me with ADD often resulting in saying or doing something we regret. When I was placed on medication the fog began to lift and I began to "observe" myself in a very different way. I noticed how difficult I made life for those around me and myself. Recently I met a woman at a meeting. She told me she would not be using her apartment in Paris, France and I could use it at no cost. I said yes. I was so happy. Imagine being in Paris in the summer.

> The following morning I made these notes:
> I knew the woman for a few hours
> Is the apartment safe?
> Does anyone else have a key to the apartment?
> I do not speak French
> I could easily get lost in Paris—bringing on an anxiety attack or even disassociation.

I am a person who thinks on paper. By doing the above and with skills I have learned, and most of all **medication**, I was able to prevent what could have been a disaster for me.

Some people do not take ADD seriously; perhaps it is because it often comes with a companion illness, in my case manic depression. ADD is not an easy illness to diagnose. Blame for the behavior is often placed on the individual. It takes a skilled psychologist or psychiatrist to diagnose. Then after careful evaluation a decision is made as to the medicine prescribed.

There is a lot of controversy about giving medication for ADD. Without the medication there is little chance for improvement. There seems to be some confusion among parents and teachers. Most psychiatrists prescribe a stimulant which when given to the average person would make him hyperactive. However, children with ADD calm down when they are treated in this manner.

JIM

In 1996 I began to realize I was in serious trouble. Between 1994 to 1996 I had 22 jobs. I was used to working in sales but I know longer lacked the 'push' to make me a desirable candidate. I was also a trainer, a position I excelled in, however there were very few companies using trainers. Two of the companies that employed me went out of business. I felt worthless when a discount chain store let me go because I was too slow at the register. I did not know what to do.

My mother who had been lending me money said I must re-file for disability. (I had applied in 1994 and was declined.) I knew nothing about getting an attorney, so I filled out the papers myself.

My mother and I agreed she would pay my expenses and I would pay her the back from the award money. I asked my mother what would happen if I weren't found disabled? She laughed. "Any one can tell you're mental," she said. My mother was enjoying this conversation too much, but I had no alternatives.

In March of 1996 I had emergency gall bladder surgery, thus burdening me with more financial obligations. I was afraid I might lose my condo. My mother paid the surgeon $800, but the rest of the bills were my problem. The phone rang constantly.

Bill paying by my mother suddenly got very chaotic and each bill had to be discussed over and over with her. The first bill I sent her was from the cable company .My mother refused to pay it. She said I didn't need cable TV. I explained the condo has no master antenna. I would not have TV. In the meantime the delinquency fee was added. Every bill received the same response from her. My car was in the repair shop and the bill was $150. She told me I didn't need a car. I should take the bus. Most of the places I needed to drive to could not be reached by bus.

In the meantime I got a booth at the flea market and started selling some of my belongings, antiques, accent pieces, lamps and pictures. The man in the next booth told me his name was Jim and if I needed to leave my booth he would be glad to watch it. We chattered for a few minutes until we both were busy. He left his booth around noon and asked me to watch it. He came back with a pizza and some cokes for us. I got a better look at him. He was tall, about 300 pounds. He told me the booth was his son's and he was helping him for the day.

After the flea market closed he helped me pack up the few things I didn't sell. He invited me for coffee. He was anxious to talk. His wife had just divorced him and had married the next week.

He still loved her and missed her. Then came my turn to down load. I told him about everything and how so late in life I had nothing and no future. He asked me who my attorney was and I told him I didn't have one. He explained to me that this was a must. "You only pay them if you win. Meet me here Monday at 9:00 a.m. and I'll get you set up with a good lawyer." I met him Monday morning and got into his Mercedes. We drove across the bridge to Tampa and that is how I met Mr. Kaye.

Several days later Jim called me and told me he had paid the cable till the end of the year. We went to dinner twice a week and he usually gave me money, however I still found it necessary to sell more and more of my things. My mother was still paying my bills at random. I started seeing more of Jim and he helped me financially. I continued to sell my belongings. I still did not know what Jim did, but he seemed to have plenty of money. I met his mother briefly and she told me Jim was mentally and physically ill. I thought this was a typical response of a mother who wants to keep her son to herself. This was not the case. As the months passed Jim became nasty. He said the only thing wrong with me was my lack of trust in God. He thought I needed to have him and his brethren perform a Deliverance. We will free you from Satan's power, trust me this is the only way I will keep seeing you. And the only way you will be well.

The night before the Deliverance was to take place Jim went through my books and music and discarded everything he was sure God did not want me to have in my home. On a late fall afternoon I found my self in the law office on one of Jim's friends. There were six men present. I told Jim I would be more comfortable if there were some women present at the Deliverance. It started and I became overwhelmed as each one talked about my personal life as if he knew me. Jim had betrayed everything I told him in confidence. I never said anything. I never cried. I was certain this was the goal. I decided to answer their questions with yes and no and I don't recall. After an hour they were nowhere near braking me and they were running out of things to ask me. They decided to lay hands on me so I could be forgiven. The group broke up slowly and I waited outside by Jim's car.

Jim was very angry. "You don't want to be healed," he said. "I don't want to be verbally gang banged by a bunch preacher. Are you a preacher I asked?" "I was until a few years ago when I was asked to leave for misappropriation of funds. I never saw Jim after this but it reminded me of my belief system and how after years it was still rooted in some mystical God who would make everything okay. The way to make everything ok is to find a good psychiatrist and work with him until you find the best combination of medications and take it every day. Stay away from all the faith healers some are just misguided and some are criminals. I have walked this path when by sense of reality was not very clear. This is the only time it made sense.

ATTORNEY KAYE

My second meeting with Mr. Kaye was very brief. He looked at my medical records. "When did you originally file?" he asked. "In 1994," I said. "Are you sure you're mentally ill," he asked. All he needed to do was read my doctor's reports. I was confused. Why does he have a negative view about my getting disability? "Well, you just don't look mentally ill," he said.

"Would it help if I looked like a bag lady," I replied. "Probably," he said, as he stood up to let me know the meeting was over.

As I was driving back to Clearwater I determined this whole disability idea was not worth it. I would start looking for work again. The hell with it, I'm getting a job with benefits. I was entitled to $600 month Social Security. How could anyone exist on it?

I started working for a large advertising company. They were very impressed with my ability and my manager took me to meet the president in Tampa. The job was not as professional as other jobs I had, but I could pay my bills. I was very happy and relaxed. My productivity was good.

A few weeks after I started this job Mr. Kaye called and told me the Judge had approved my disability request without a hearing based on the information provided by my psychologist and my psychiatrist. I told him I would have to decline. I found a job I liked and I would rather work. He was very impressed. We agreed to drop the claim.

About three weeks later I woke up shaking and crying. I dragged myself to work. The next few weeks I experienced a chemical depression. I forgot which file to use on the computer. I could not keep up with the rotating phone line making it necessary for someone else to do part of my work. While I was never a good speller, I now could not remember even simple words. The pricing, even with a calculator, was confusing as I struggled to remember the price formula. After about two weeks of this depression the manager met me at the door. She gave me a box with the contents of my desk in it and told me I was not the kind of person they wanted to work there.

ATTORNEY KAYE—THE HEARING

I called Mr. Kaye to find out the status of my disability file and told him what had happened and I had made a terrible mistake. He looked grim at our next meeting and informed me my file had been sent back. The best we could hope for was a hearing.

In June 1997, I got a letter informing me of my Hearing date, July 8, 1997. I asked Mr. Kaye if I could bring my psychologist to the hearing. "That won't be necessary," said Mr. Kaye. I asked him if I should dress a certain way? "No," he said.

I got my things together for the hearing. I wore a simple green dress I had for years. It was pressed and clean. I wore pantyhose and brown shoes that were neither old nor new. I blew dry my hair after I had showered. I looked respectable. I was soon to learn you don't go to a disability hearing looking respectable.

The hearing itself was over in less than forty minutes. The Judge was a heavy man and his cheeks were flush. I thought he resembled Santa Claus. He was very friendly and asked me about my average day. I had been working for so many years I didn't have an average day.

He asked me if I could cook to which I replied, "Yes." I then made a very bad mistake I told him I went to the library to check out videos. I actually believed as a judge he would know people suffering from mental illness, especially panic attacks were encourage to watch videos to help them overcome this time of distress.

My Attorney said nothing except for some opening remarks. He never mentioned my 22 jobs in the last two years. The Judge told us the hearing was over. Mr. Kaye and I talked briefly and then parted. I felt everything would be all right, after all the judge had the statements from my psychologist saying I was disabled as well as my psychiatrist's report, both felt strongly I needed to stop working.

The only other doctor I had seen was a doctor from India at Directions in Mental Health. I went here to receive some of my medication at no cost. This doctor's function was to monitor my medication. I saw him every three months or a total of four visits. This psychiatrist wrote pages about me and none of it based on fact. He even went so far as to write glowing reports about my physical appearance, which I consider, crossing the line. I continued to see my psychiatrist and psychologist and never had any conversations with this doctor for fear of having my medications changed. However, the Judge would make this doctor the "treating physician" and his nonsense would prevail.

DECISION—THEN APPEAL

I waited impatiently for the Decision. I was almost certain it had been awarded. My doctor's statement were accurate and expressed my difficulties in trying to hold a job when experiencing mood swings, panic attacks and abandonment issues, plus disassociation.

In October of 1997, the Decision was mailed to me. It awarded me back disability until I saw the doctor from India who said I was in remission. A doctor who knew nothing about me and had seen me for all of one hour combined was now being called **the treating physician**. The information taken for fact is always the **treating physician's**. I had seen my psychiatrist and my psychologist for a total of eight years and continued to do so.

The judge had the gall to say my psychiatrist, "greatly inflated his findings." How he knew this is a mystery to me. This is the same as lying. Does a judge have the right to make such a prejudicial statement? The Decision was disjointed, unclear, full of provable mistakes. It was obvious no one with any intelligence wrote it.

What this meant to me was I would no longer be considered disabled or as the Judge put it I was in "remission." Remission is for cancer not mental illness that grows more challenging with time.

My attorney thought this was a "fair" decision and would not represent me in an appeal. I don't know if he really thought this to be a fair decision or his $4000 earnings for representing me would be paid at this time, but not for the appeal, win or lose it.

I consider this to be the one of the best thing to happen to me, because with Mr. Kaye representing me at the appeal I would certainly have lost. He did not believe there was anything wrong with me, although he never voiced it. He should have refused my case if he could not give a better defense than he did.

Now came the real work, the appeal. I had called about ten lawyers in the area. All of them asked me about my appearance in court. When I told them they declined to take the case. Most attorneys told me I should have gone two days without a shower, not combed my hair, brushed my teeth and worn my worst clothes. In the beginning I would challenge them but it became apparent that for the mentally ill a hearing means a costume party. This is so degrading. We have to dress up like street people to be awarded disability, which if we don't get will make us street people. I've known far more mentally ill people who dressed like their piers than Street. People. Almost all the attorneys told me to drop the case and re-file. I was certain to get a different judge. I was also certain to lose all the back disability from 1994. I had sacrificed too much to give up now.

When I talked to attorneys the question was always, "Who was the judge?" When I told them I was informed he was the most difficult of the thirteen judges and he seldom gave a reversal. The procedure is for the Appeal Board to review the case and send it back to the original judge if they think it has merit. In a small minority of cases they overrule the judge. No attorney wanted my case. In January 1999, I went down to the courthouse and filed my own appeal. By now I was so familiar with the case it was not hard to do.

I continued looking for an attorney to take the appeal. In March I found one. He was a very nice and caring man, about forty. He seemed to understand mental illness and did not treat me as though I was retarded or someone to be feared. We discussed a plan, things I should fax him and I felt encouraged for first time in months.

I had to get some money and the last things I sold were heartbreakers. My children's christening clothes, Staffordshire ware which I had collected over a period of 20 years, china dishes, linens, my Thomasville dining room chairs, art I had collected over the years and all my jewelry. I still was going without food part of the time and making a meal out of Gatorade

My attorney suggested I go to Social Services in Clearwater. I felt sick of the thought of going on welfare. It was even worse than I imagined. I enter a room filled with a sea of black faces and learned what it meant to be a minority. All the workers were black and I still had not mastered the art of "dressing poor." Most of the people wore jeans and had several children with them. I was one of the older women there. I waited until my name was called. The worker was a tall thin black woman who eyed me suspiciously. She gave me a list of official documents to bring to our next meeting. I noticed she had many Christian clippings and pictures taped to her wall. At our next meeting I brought every thing she asked for which meant I would be eligible for some help with my mortgage and help will several prescriptions. The following month she said I had not brought in all my papers, so I could not receive aid this month. I had brought in all the official papers required, but she would claim I was missing something I had already had shown her. It was a game.

The next month I brought all the papers again. She began the paper work. A portion of my mortgage was paid, but always late eventually throwing my condo into default. There was nothing I could do about this but I was now more than ever determined to receive the benefits of all the tax dollars I had spent in my life.

The next method of torment revolved around the appointment time. I would always arrive before my appointment and this caseworker would pull my file and put it on her desk. An average of two hours would go by before she would call me. Walk-ins were supposed to be seen after people with an appointment, but they were taken ahead of me. Finally she would take me, but always insist I hadn't brought all the necessary papers. After this I brought everyone with me each time I went to Social Services. One time my income was two dollars too high to receive my medicine. After she told me she sat back in her chair and waited for me to say something. I did not say a word. She broke the silence by asking me if I was a Christian? After silence on my part I knew I had to say yes to get the medicine, so I did. This is the danger of Christianity. It invites one to assume the role of God when they are talking or working with someone they feel is unsaved and in some weird way think they are pleasing God.

The worst was still come. I decided to change my appointment times to mornings to avoid having to stay till closing because I was being discrimination against. Mornings are a difficult time for me and going to Social Service in the morning was an even more difficult. There were a lot more people in the waiting room and the television was blaring. Mothers were yelling at their children. I began to realize I was about to lose my hearing. I saw the supervisor, Mr. Green, and told him I was about to lose my hearing, I needed to go to an empty office. He said, "no way you're just trying to get ahead of everyone." "This is a disability," I said and then my hearing was gone and I burst in to tears. He took me back to the break room and my hearing came back gradually. My worker came to the break room and told me I would have to bring someone with me next time because I could not control my behavior.

I could not find anyone. I didn't have any friends and I did not want any of my neighbors to know. My daughter had made it clear she wanted nothing to do with me during this period. "It was too negative." However, she could have been an important help for me with Social Services. She is both rational and intimidating. My son lived in Boston so he was out of the question. I called about six of the mental health agencies and they informed me they were not geared for this situation.

I called my attorney and he said he would speak with the person in charge of Social Service. He accompanied me to my next appointment. He asked to speak to the Director. At first he was met with some resistance from the worker but she backed down. Ms. Andrews came to the office and my attorney told and showed her what has transpired. After this visit I had few problems with Social Service.

EDUARDO

I had just gotten comfortable on my lounge chair by the condo pool when I heard the scrape of another lounge chair being put into position. I looked over and saw the most drop-dead handsome man I had ever seen except for Ricardo Montalban and Enzio Pinza. "Good morning," he said with a slight trace of a Spanish accent. We talked small talk because every time we would get to talking about what is important to us he talked a bout politics in South America, something I knew nothing about or I came very close to telling him about the Appeal. I had come to look at everyone as a potential savior.

He invited me to swim with him and I did. Our conversation was less serious in the water. He told me his name was Eduardo and I introduced myself. He had been a pilot for a major airline and was retired. At times I had trouble following the conversation, not because of his accent but because his body was so perfect. I was distracted to by the grace with which he moved.

I was hoping this would lead to something and at the same time afraid it would. I had nothing to worry about. Two months had past and I had not seen Eduardo. He was not by the pool and I had no idea in which of the ten buildings he lived. Perhaps he had moved. I had stopped going to the pool when the weather changed. It seemed futile to me to search for him. It should be the other way around.

Florida usually doesn't gets very cold, but you are keenly aware of the weather when it does. I had gone for a walk and decided to cut it short when I heard my name being called. I was so happy. It was Eduardo. He put his arm around me and held me close. It was as if we had known each other forever. "Come let's go for coffee," he said. I thought of my work on the appeal but decided to go.

He told me he was called back to South America on short notice because his eldest brother was dying. "I was with him when he died," Eduardo said. He went on to talk about the values of his former country comparing them to ours. "A family is the most important part of life, but here in America it is different." I did not mention the appeal. We did not need the appeal killing this relationship before it got started.

He said, "We must go to dinner tonight and celebrate our friendship." I agreed. He took me to a lovely Spanish Restaurant. After the meal we walked in the courtyard and Eduardo took my hand and we sat down. He told me about his childhood. It had been a happy one and as he talked I began to understand his need for independence.

I said little about myself except that I had been born in New York City. He was pleased by this information. "I think people from big cities have an advantage over others. New York City has always fascinated me," he said. We stood up and walked over to the fountain. "May I kiss you?" he asked. I whispered, "Yes." In the dim light I could see his hazel blue eyes and the next moment we were embracing and kissing. I felt light-headed. It was like a movie. In my head I could hear the music to, *Some Enchanted Evening*, and I thought this must be the most romantic evening of my life.

FINAL APPEAL

The appeal proved to be a test of strength for me. The sense of urgency was overwhelming and I felt my very life depended upon it, because it did. I worked day and night thinking of contacts, writing letters, making phone calls. I called people at Social Security. I faxed twelve pages of information to Hillary Clinton, but received no reply.

It was fall of 1999, and my appeal was scheduled for August of 2000, a long time away. I would lose everything even if I won. My attorney tried to move the date up by contacting the Appeal Board and writing them about my needs and the reply that came back read, "Everyone has a need."

I decided it was time to do things my way. This was an error on the part of the judge and I was going through hell because of it. I had been in contact with my Congressman's office. The woman assigned to my case was indifferent at best. She forwarded a letter from my psychologist to the Congressman to the Appeal Board. The Appeal Board had a copy, but the letter she received was meant for the Congressman. To compound matters she sent me a thank you note. Why? I tried working with the Congressman's office in Washington, but calls were never returned. When I called the Clearwater office to speak to his aid she was sick, on vacation, or gone for the day. I could see this calling and writing was going nowhere. My frustration was mounting and I knew I had to do something drastic.

I realized this was not about need, as everyone in this situation is needy, but my case was really about a judge's error. I went through his Decision and highlighted all of his mistakes. Even I was amazed at how many there were. I could demonstrate repeatedly how the doctor from Directions was not the treating physician. Every page of the Decision was attached to my back up material.

When I finished I faxed a copy to my attorney, who was horrified. "You can't say such things about a federal judge," he said. "Watch me," I said. "If you send this I'm off the case," he replied. I knew what I had to do. I put it in a large envelope and addressed the envelope. I carefully put a label on it and neatly wrote "**For the Congressman Only**" in about six places on the envelope.

I had filed my appeal in January and it was now November. After I sent the information to the Congressman I received a letter from him informing me that my case had been given to the Congressional Liaison. I was pleased, and my attorney decided he was back on the case. In a short time I was told my case was moved to Critical Care. I began to relax.

The case was ready to go to the Appeal Board when it was lost. Social Security did not have any back up. Nothing is apparently stored in a computer. The original paper files are kept in warehouses. The only process available now would be to re-file and lose everything I had already work on. I didn't know what to do. I was totally alone, except for my son who made phone calls and wrote letters on my behalf. There was no family to help or encourage me. It was as if they all left the planet. Perhaps they felt if I lost the words of Christ, "I was a stranger and you took me in," would haunt them

There was nothing to fight for any more and nothing to do. Keeping busy had helped me but now I felt this emptiness. I had gone through this horror of a life only to have some ignorant judge make an assessment based on my appearance, and not my doctor's statements about my illness. I had all but given up when a week later my attorney received word the file had been found and the Appeal Board had ruled in my favor. This is significant because the procedure is for the Appeal Board to look over the case and if it has merit give it back to the Judge to review. In my case the Appeal Board ruled in my favor because of the obvious errors on the part of the judge.

Suggestions if You Have to Appeal a Disability Decision
Find an attorney who understands Mental Illness. Classes are offered to attorneys.
Find an attorney who believes you. If they in any way imply you are a fraud, find someone else
Take an active part in your appeal.
Clear everything you do with your attorney.
Enlist the help of friends if they have contacts who can help you.
Monitor your case and know what your doctor says about you.

EDUARDO AND A TRIP TO NEW YORK CITY

The appeal kept me busy, however, now I was reminded that I had not told Eduardo about my illness. I knew I had to tell him but I liked him so much it would be hard to see him go. We had been seeing each other for two months when Eduardo announced he had purchased plane tickets and made reservations for us to stay in a hotel in New York. I did not say anything, but I was thinking that this was not good. If I were having a bad day he would not understand. I had suspected that for the last two days I was going into a depressed mode. Normally if I thought I was going to be depressed I would just make up a reason not to see him for a few days.

We left for New York the following Friday. Eduardo was happy as we boarded the plane. I was starting to feel weak and irritable. He turned to me and said, "Now you can show me your New York." I thought, what does he think I am some goddamn tour guide. I knew I was in trouble.

When we were in the air he asked me if I knew the way to *Tavern on the Green*. "Yes," I snapped. "You hail a cab and tell the driver you want to go to *Tavern on the Green*". "I see," he said, and then he waited until after dinner before he spoke to me. I did not want to talk. I wanted to sleep in a bed forever.

"Is there something wrong?" he asked. "No," I said in a whisper. I did not want to try and explain it to him in this state of mind. It was dark when we arrived. We took a cab to the hotel and my plans were to go to bed and try not to cry. Eduardo was happy and excited. I was angry. The room was not as clean as it should be. There was a burned out light bulb in the bathroom and the towels were well worn. "Why did you bring me to this hotel? It's awful, "I said. I wasn't sure if he was angry or confused. He said nothing for about twenty minutes and that made me angry. "Are you going to talk to me?" I asked. He remained silent. I threw my shoes at him and anything I could grab. He ducked and kept from being hit. "Who are you he asked, some demon from hell?" "Oh, I'm more than that. I have a brain that goes crazy whenever it feels like it. All right, I have a chemical imbalance in my brain and every so often I get depressed or manic

depending on the serotonin level in my brain. I'm sorry I ruined your trip."
"Don't worry about the trip," he replied. "We will do what ever it takes to make
you comfortable. In the morning we will have breakfast in the room and you can
tell me more about these demons who possess you." I stopped crying and he held
my hand till I fell asleep. By morning the agitated depression seemed to dissipate
and I was full of remorse. I cried during breakfast while Eduardo read the paper.
When he put the paper down he took my hand in his and smiled. "How do you
feel?" he asked. I felt so guilty about the night before I started to cry. "Is there
something you would like to do," he asked. "Tell me what you would like to do,
and if you are up to it we can try." He suggested the Metropolitan Museum of
Art. He picked it because I had told him how much I liked to go there. We
dressed casually and took a cab to the museum. I was still on the verge of tears
but able to control myself. I was hoping this would be a mood swing that would
dissipate quickly and we could still have some fun. We did. We had dinner at the
Tavern on the Green. I looked at this good looking man across the table from me
and felt sadness. He would leave like the others. We enjoyed ourselves that
evening, but it would all soon be a memory.

STREET PEOPLE

WHO ARE THEY, WHERE DID THEY COME FROM, WHO IS RESPONSIBLE?

While Street People are often frightening it is important to remember they are the one who are frightened. The majority of these people were once in institutions where they were given food and shelter, and had their medicines monitored. It was a sterile life, but they had the basics. These people were not able to care for themselves. When you consider that often a mentally ill person has one or maybe two mentally ill parents it is obvious his family home is not the place for him. However the Reagan Administration had a "better idea." Reagan always had budget problems and this would be a better way to solve some of his budget problems—close all or most of the mental institutions and send these poor people back to their loved ones.

Unable to cope with relatives they left and began wandering the streets. They gathered together where there was grass to put down newspapers so they could sleep at night. I saw this in San Francisco, New York and Tampa. This is supposed to be a compassionate country, sending millions of dollars in aid abroad only to allow our own sick people to wander the streets without proper clothing, to go without meals and medications.

This is the true legacy of the Reagan administration. They "saved" money in the most cowardly way.

WHICH OF THESE FOUR PEOPLE IS MENTALLY ILL?

THE HOMELESS PERSON

HELPFUL SUGGESTIONS

The following suggestions have helped me survive some of the difficult times by preventing or not aggravating my position on the tight rope of day to day living with Manic Depression or ADD.

Manic depression is usually at its worst for me during the first few hours of the morning. I sit in semi darkness drinking my tea and wonder if this will be a dark day. If I have an appointment I organize around it. Will I be up to showering and dressing? Minor things often upset me. To prevent the morning from becoming too complicated I start the previous night. I walk through my home picking up any cups, glasses, magazines, or other items. I straighten up the house, but not clean it.

I write my to do list, a must if you have ADD and necessary with manic depression. I am usually in a fog in the morning and if I have only one paper to guide me life gets bearable. I make the list of every thing I have to do. I divide the list into subtitles called, *Places to go*, *Things to purchase*, *Telephone calls to make*, and *If there is time and I am feeling up to the task*:

> *Places to go*
> 11:00 a.m.: Dr. James (remember to ask about the lab test)
>
> *Things to purchase*
> Birthday card for Sue
>
> *People to call*
> Mary
> Bank
>
> *If there is time and I am feeling up to the task*
> Dusting
> Change sheets

You may not be able to do all of the items on the list on the *If there is time* section, so start with the one you prefer.

Very important! Try to avoid toxic people. These are the people you know who upset you consciously on subconsciously. They are people who say things with double meanings when they talk to you. For example, they might say, "You look so nice. I didn't think people on Social Security could afford something nice." Or, "Oh, I forgot you shop at thrift stores. I always wanted to see what they were like. But you know my husband forbids me to go. He seems to think those stores are for street people."

There is no civilized reply to this kind of toxic remark. Try to avoid people like this and if you know they are going to be at a gathering you are invited to it is really best to stay home. That's why headaches were invented, as last minute excuses. It has been my experience that this toxicity can be 'infectious,' forcing me to stay in bed for days.

Shopping tips! There are times when I am too optimistic (mania) and these are the times I love to shop. I pull out the credit cards and spend. After an incident in Tampa several years ago I came up with some shopping rules for myself. At this cute little trendy shop I purchased clothes that did not fit my lifestyle, as they were for someone twenty years younger than I. I was so excited about "the new me." Several days later when I looked at what I had purchased I began to cry. I would never wear these teenage clothes. I looked at the receipt, which read, "All Sales are Final." Maybe they won't be so bad once I try them on I thought. Needless to say they were worse than I thought, a lot worse. I looked like a punk rocker.

I made some rules for myself. I only shop at stores allowing me a thirty days to bring the item back. During this time period the clothes hang in my closet for two weeks. I then take a look at them and if I still like them I try them on. If it passes this test I keep it. If I find it is anywhere from 'off the wall' to 'not quite right' I return it. I never return clothes I've worn.

Most of my clothes do not come from department stores. My budget is very tight. I have discovered thrift stores, which not only helps my budget, but also helps feed what I call the 'hunter' part of ADD. I move through the stores slowly looking for anything that might have been put on the wrong size rack. I have found some of my best items this way. Many thrift shops have days when all clothing is marked half price. If you can make friends with someone who works or volunteers at you favorite store you might be able to find out those sale dates in advance.

Tips for traveling with medications. Please, don't call them drugs. It makes you sound like a space cadet. If you are using any mode of transportation except your own car keep your medicines with you. Carry it in the original bottles, especially if you are flying out of the country. If you can carry it in your purse, do so. However, if you are like me, and have a lot of medicine put it in your carry on luggage.

On one of my business trips to Dallas for a trade show, the limousine did not have enough room for everyone and we had to squeeze together. My manager saw my carry on bag on my lap and snatched it from me. "This belongs in the trunk," she said. I had a sinking feeling. We registered and then I saw the bellhop and the luggage cart. I quickly walked to the luggage cart, but my carry on bag was not there. During the next two hours I played '*Monkey in the Middle*', with the limousine company and the hotel. Each one claimed the other was responsible. I went to my room and started to cry. I could not go a whole week without medicine. Mary was my roommate, as usual. She was very kind. She made some phone calls and the bag was delivered by the bellhop. Thanks to her kindness I was able to get through the week. **You are responsible for your medications**. The best action for me to have taken was to get out of the limousine, get my bags and take a cab to the hotel.

CONCLUSION

Three years ago the Food and Drug Administration approved a new medicine for manic depression. This medication has helped my depression and limited my mood swings. It helps me achieve some peace of mind. It is not a cure. I still have mood swings. However, if you are not being helped by your present medications ask your psychiatrist about some of the newer medications.

It is very tempting to measure oneself against the accomplishments of those that are not inflicted with this disease and feel as if you have failed. I believed this about myself until I realized how much I have struggled to fight this illness most of my life. It has taken me sixty years, but with medication I have I have attained a measure of peace and acceptance of myself.

In the last four decades I have seen so many positive changes in the treatment available for mental illness. I look forward to the day when all mentally ill people find their conditions arrested and can lead a life of dignity instead of remorse for uncontrollable actions. It takes character to fight this illness. It takes courage to get out of bed each day. It takes courage not to surrender to the desire to end one's life.

0-595-28905-3